ABANDONED NORTHERN CALIFORNIA

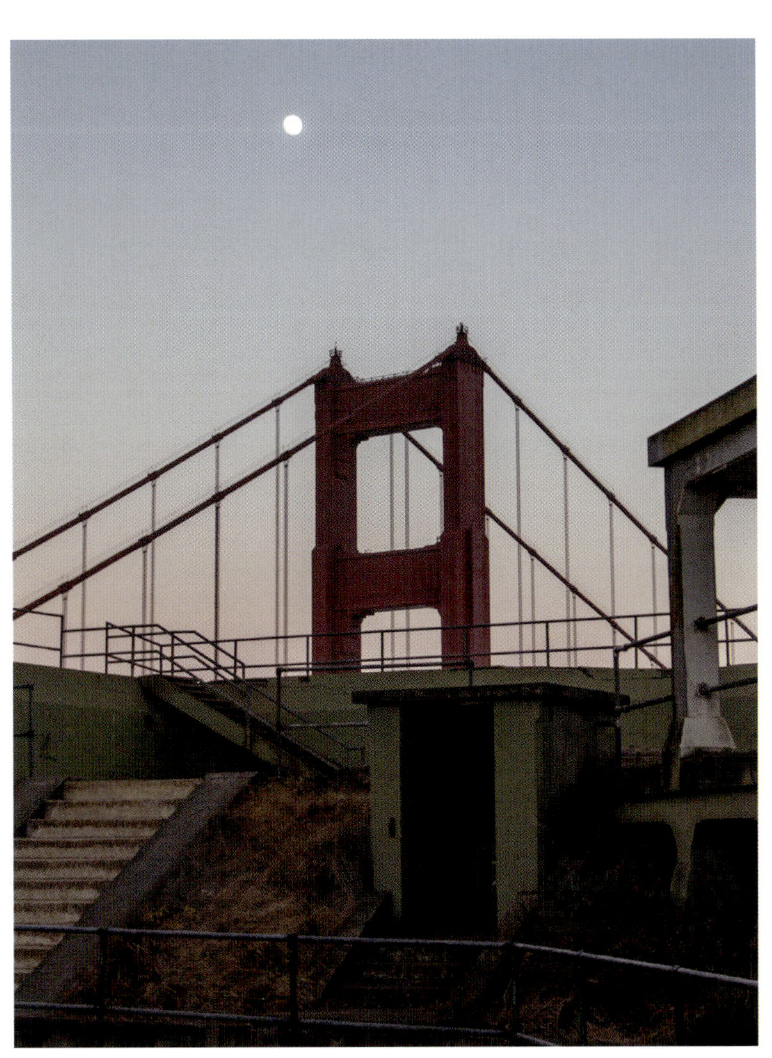

ABANDONED NORTHERN CALIFORNIA

A LAND OF CONTRADICTIONS

JOANNA KALAFATIS

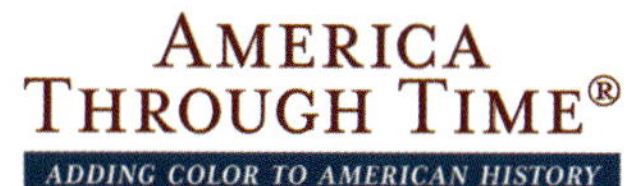

America Through Time is an imprint of Fonthill Media LLC
www.through-time.com
office@through-time.com

Published by Arcadia Publishing by arrangement with Fonthill Media LLC
For all general information, please contact Arcadia Publishing:
Telephone: 843-853-2070
Fax: 843-853-0044
E-mail: sales@arcadiapublishing.com
For customer service and orders:
Toll-Free 1-888-313-2665

www.arcadiapublishing.com

First published 2018

ISBN 978-1-63499-091-2

Typeset in Trade Gothic 10pt on 15pt
Printed and bound in England

ACKNOWLEDGMENTS

The travel and research I undertook to create this book has been an unforgettable experience; from the long road trip throughout central and northern California to document these abandoned landmarks, to the research I did into this amazing state's history, the intriguing story of Northern California has fascinated me. The travel preparation, research, development, and publication of *Abandoned Northern California* would not have been possible without the support of many incredible people around me, including relatives, friends, as well as great mentors and teachers of photography.

I would first like to thank my wonderful parents, John and Maria, who nurtured my love of exploration and historic places a long time ago and have supported me in all my endeavors. In addition, I would also like to thank the numerous friends who accompanied me on endless road trips, excursions, and hiking journeys to explore some of my favorite abandoned destinations, including several featured in this book. Special thanks go to my dear friend Vicky, who somehow lasted eight days in a campervan next to me dealing with dirt roads, getting lost in the mountains, and sleeping in bear territory, to mention just a few of our on-the-road experiences, all to explore abandoned locations and some of the most remote areas in California.

I would additionally like to extend my gratitude to all the wonderful California natives in my life, who tipped me off to some of these mesmerizing locations, and transferred to me their unconditional love for their home state. Special thanks should also be given to JUCY, the company who gave me the campervan that became my home and transportation for eight days while on this journey.

Most importantly, I would like to thank Jay Slater, Alan Sutton, and Kena Longabaugh, Fonthill Media, and Arcadia Publishing, who gave me the opportunity to write, organize, and publish a book on one of my favorite photography topics.

ABOUT THE AUTHOR

JOANNA KALAFATIS is a travel writer and actress based in Los Angeles. She has previously lived in New York and Greece, and traveled to over thirty-five countries. After obtaining her B.A. in Economics from Barnard College, she decided to apply herself to her creative pursuits. Her articles have appeared in several online and print publications, and she also writes on her travel blog, LosetheMap.com. Joanna has a deep love for and fascination with her adopted state, and is always trying to learn as much as possible about the history and experience of California.

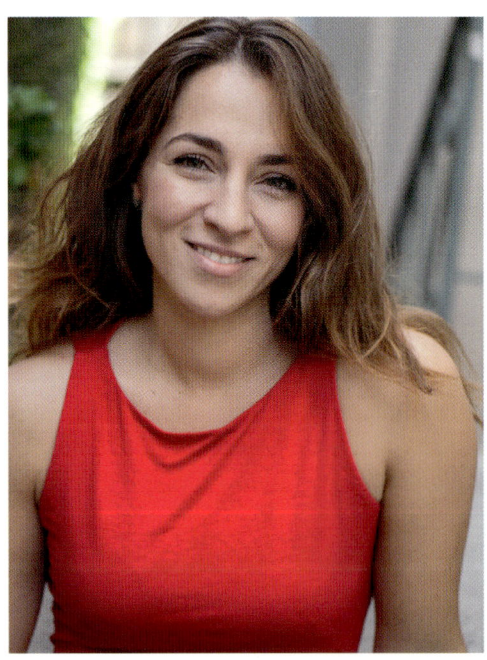

CONTENTS

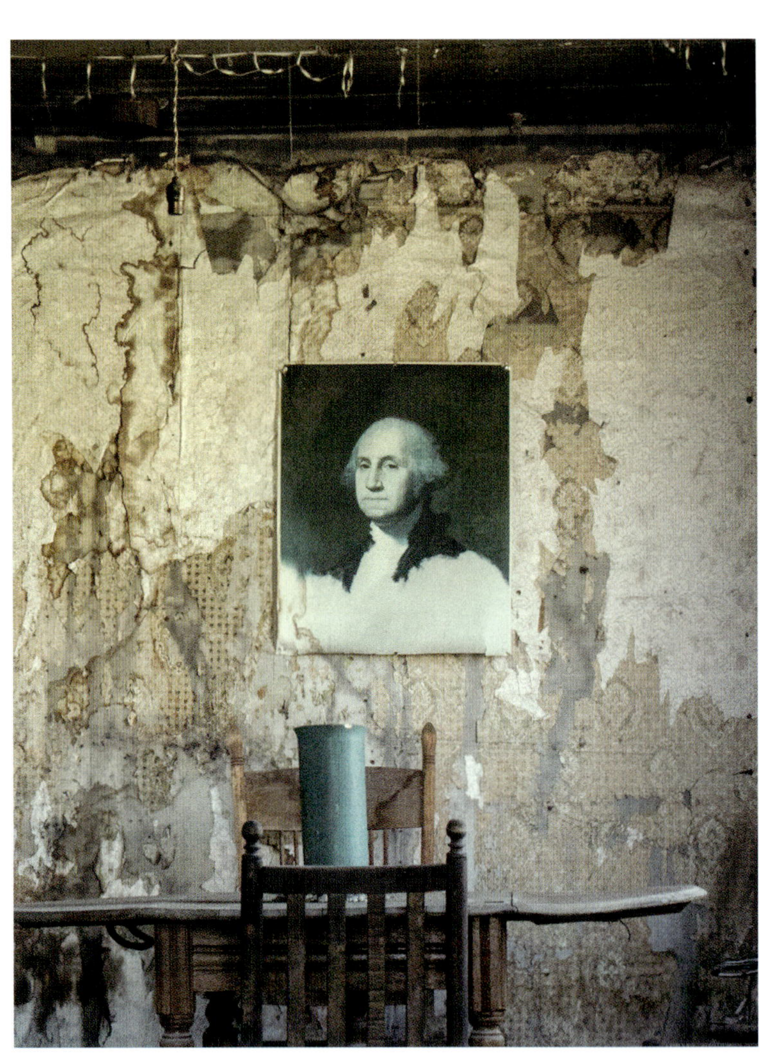

INTRODUCTION

Northern California is a land of contradictions. Just a few miles from towering mountains and forests that block out the sky you will find arid deserts and marshes. Within a few hours' drive, you will pass poor, rural towns located in some of the most inhospitable corners of the state, luxurious countryside manors in the wine country, and major US centers of business and technology, including the most expensive city in the country. Yes, it's San Francisco.

These intriguing differences result from both the variety of nature and conditions to be found in this part of California, as well as the diverse types of people that settled there over the years. From gold prospectors and fishermen to brilliant inventors and writers, to the entrepreneurs who would become the titans of the wine industry, an unimaginable range of people and forces shaped the modern environment of Northern California.

This diversity of background, lifestyle, and mindset is still evident in the multitude of abandoned buildings, towns, and wrecks left behind. By exploring these captivating ruins, we can get a better sense of how Northern California became the puzzling collection of people from all walks of life that it is today.

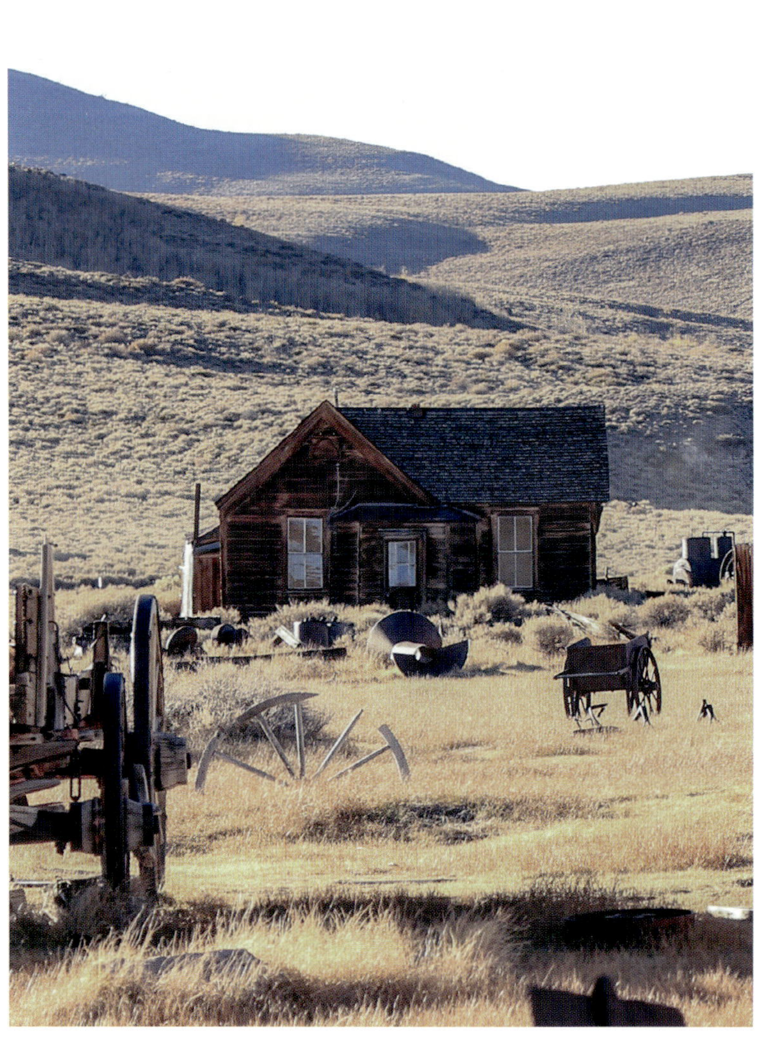

1

BODIE: PRESERVING THE OLD WEST

GOLD MINING AND OUTLAWS

The town of Bodie was built east of the Sierra Nevada Mountains of California during the gold rush, after the discovery of gold reserves nearby. Erected in one of the harshest corners of the state at an elevation of over 8,000 feet, subject to blazing heat in the summers and freezing cold in the winters, pelted by strong winds on an unprotected mountainside, with no water or wood for miles around, the residents of Bodie held on to their homes in the face of incredibly challenging conditions, all in hopes of eventual prosperity. When those hopes eventually dwindled, the population quickly, and perhaps predictably, declined.

Founded in 1859, Bodie was named after one of its discoverers, W. S. Body, shortly after his death in a winter blizzard—perhaps an omen of the area's inhospitable nature. The town's peak years came after 1975, when rich new deposits were discovered and prospectors from all over the United States came flooding into the small boomtown. Bodie's startup newspaper summed up the rapid change in the town's status best, in the following quote:

> Gold—But a few short months ago Bodie was an insignificant little place, now she is rapidly growing in size and importance and people are crowding in upon her from far and near, and why? Because of the rich discoveries of gold – yellow, glittering, precious gold.

Bodie quickly became famous not only for its mines, but also for its outlaw reputation. The town attracted young men to a hostile environment, desperately seeking wealth and riches, and often getting disappointed. Gunfights and violence became common in the streets of the once small mining town.

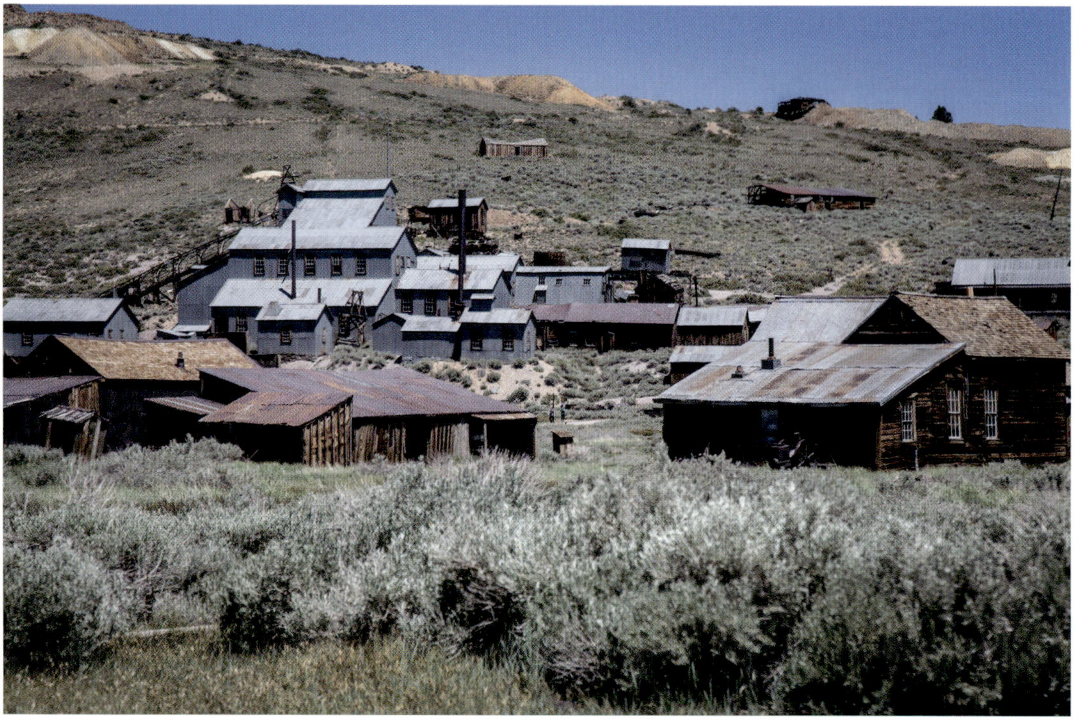

A landscape shot of Bodie with its grey-walled mining facilities.

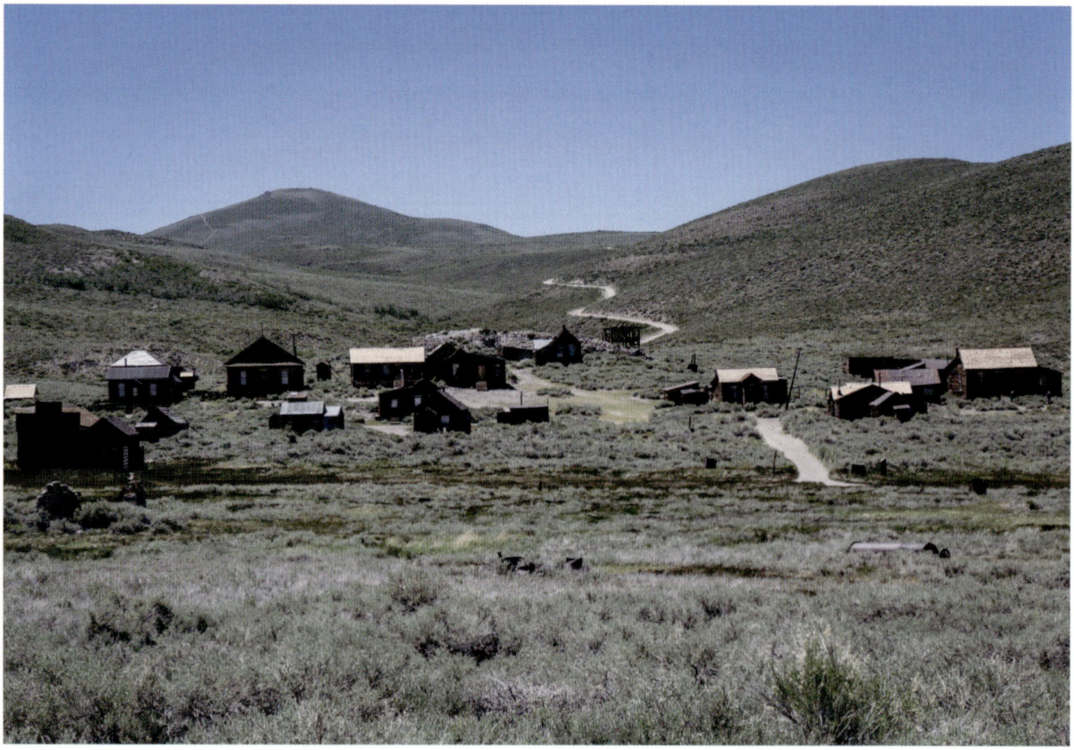

Bodie homes as seen from a distance.

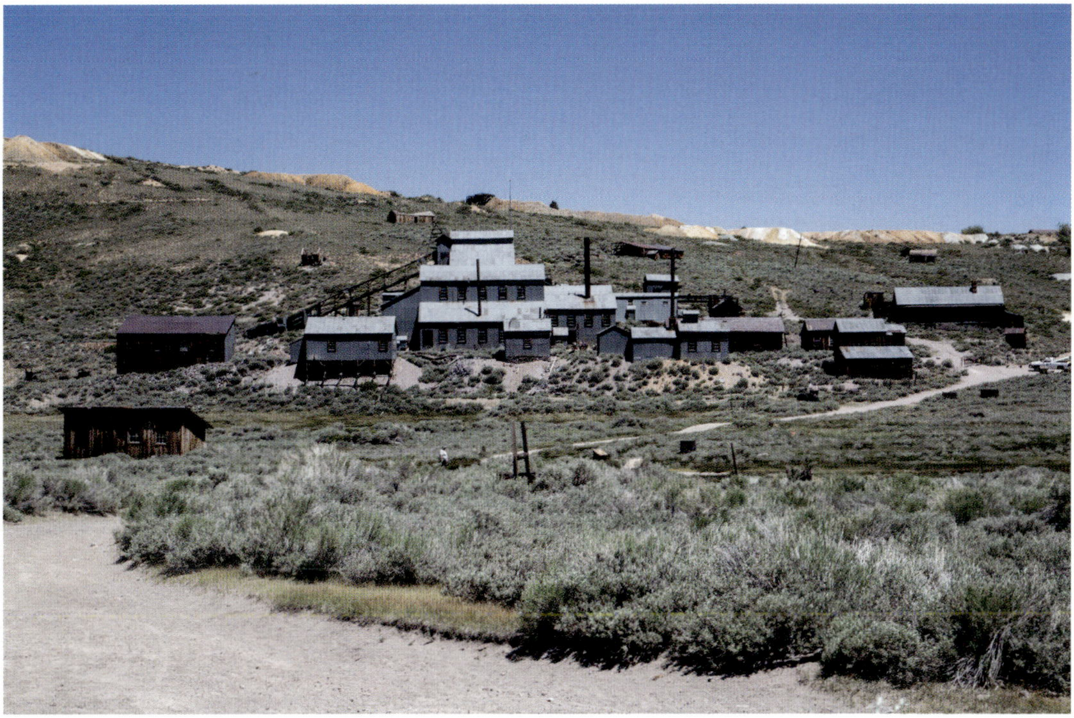

Wide shot of the Bodie mining facility.

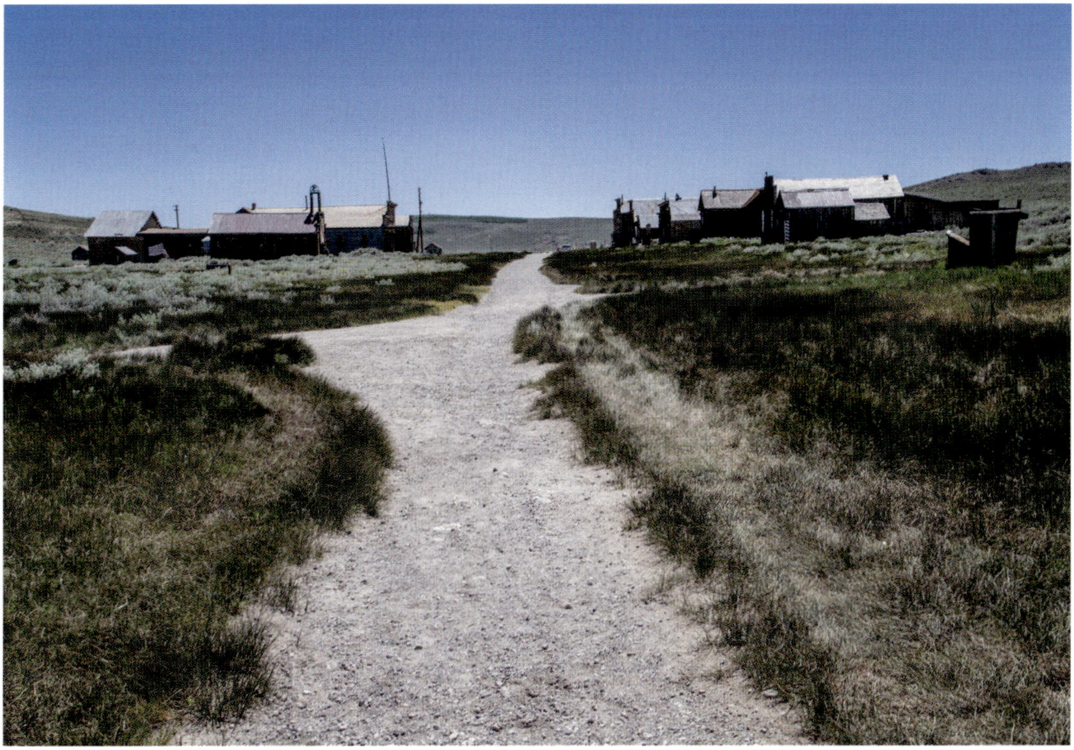

Only dirt roads lead into and out of Bodie.

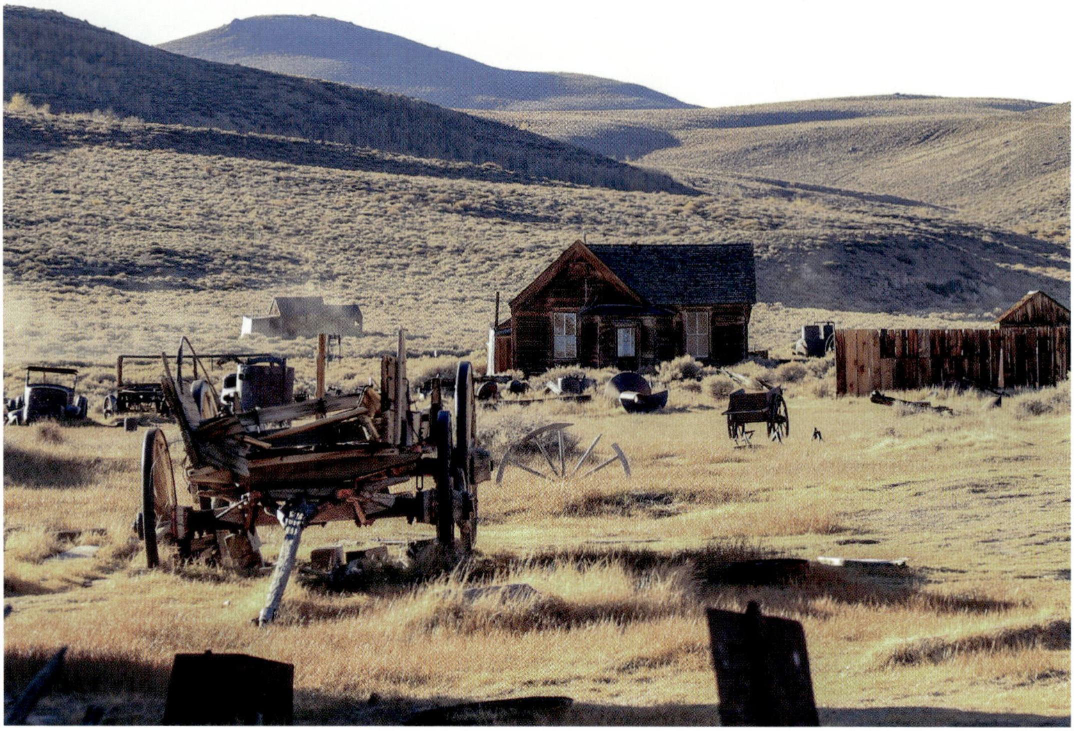

A sunset view of Bodie as the light hits the abandoned homes and wagons.

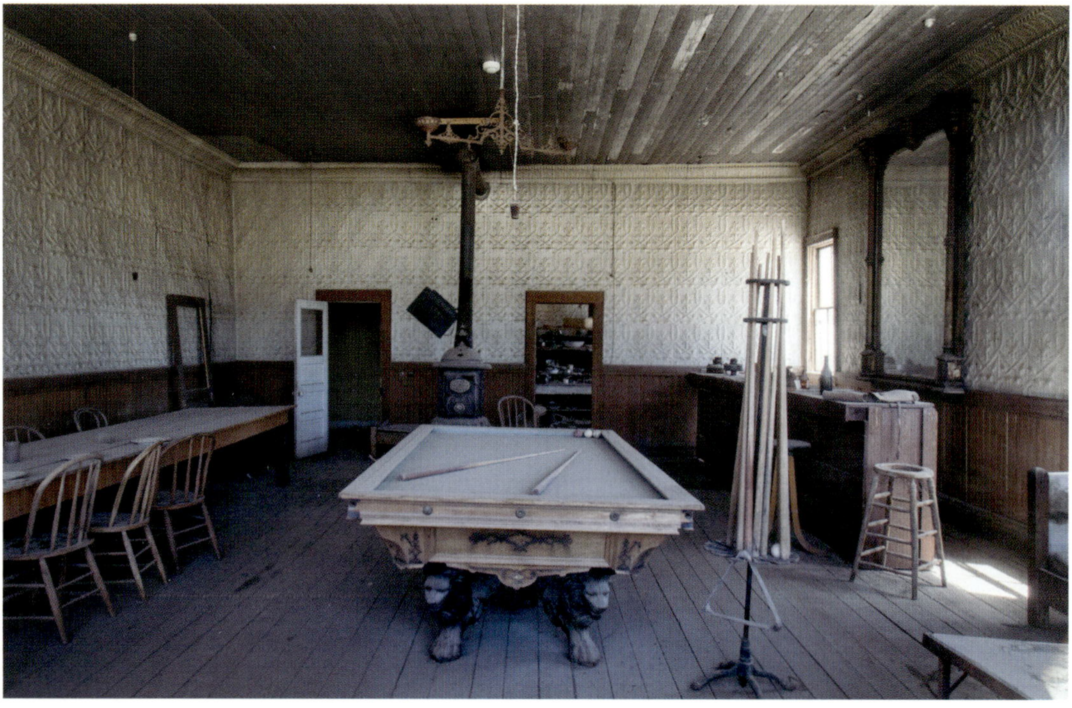

The saloon and billiard hall of a Bodie hotel.

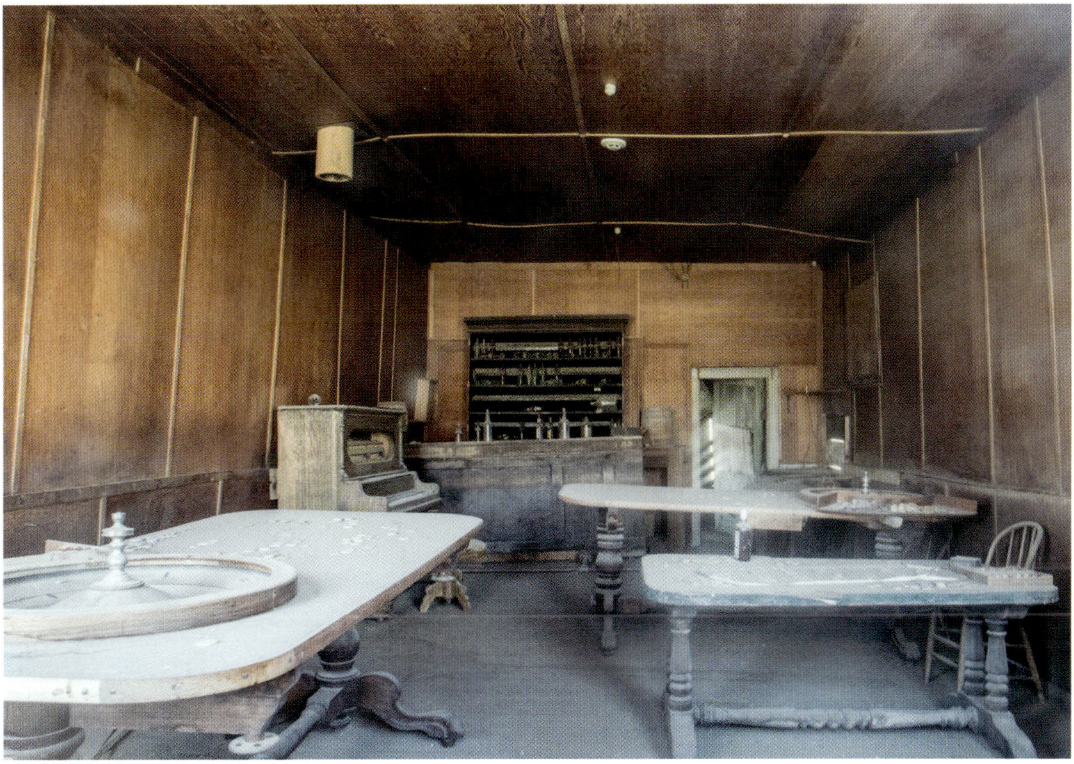

A prominent roulette table shows that this was a gambling hall.

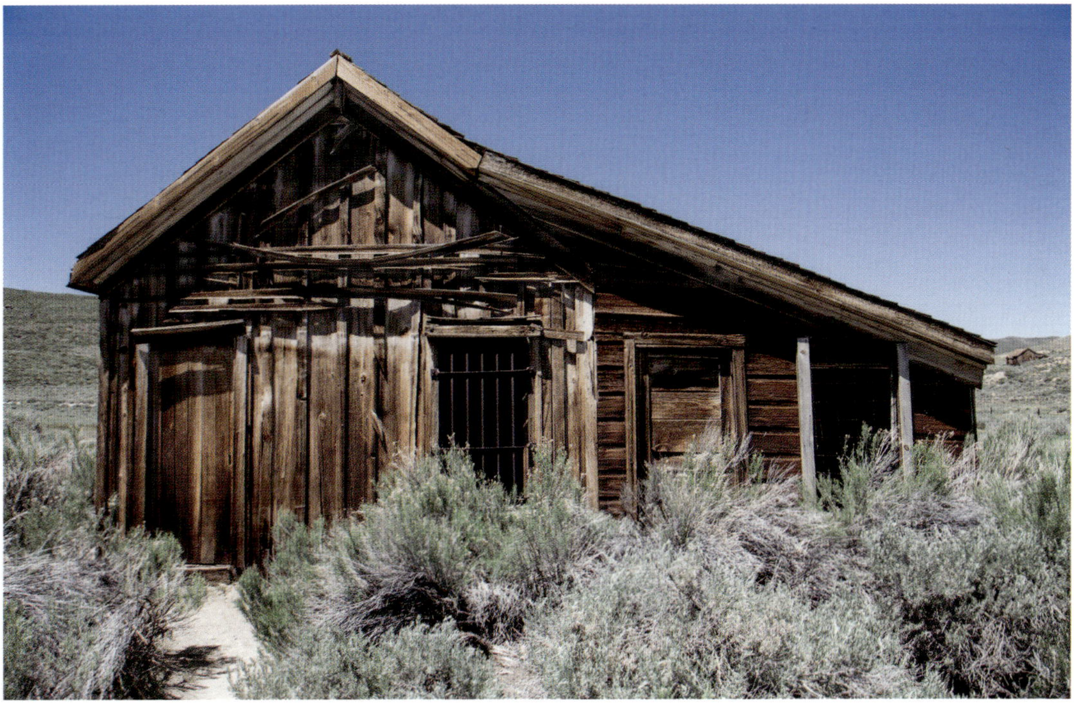

An exterior view of the local Bodie jail.

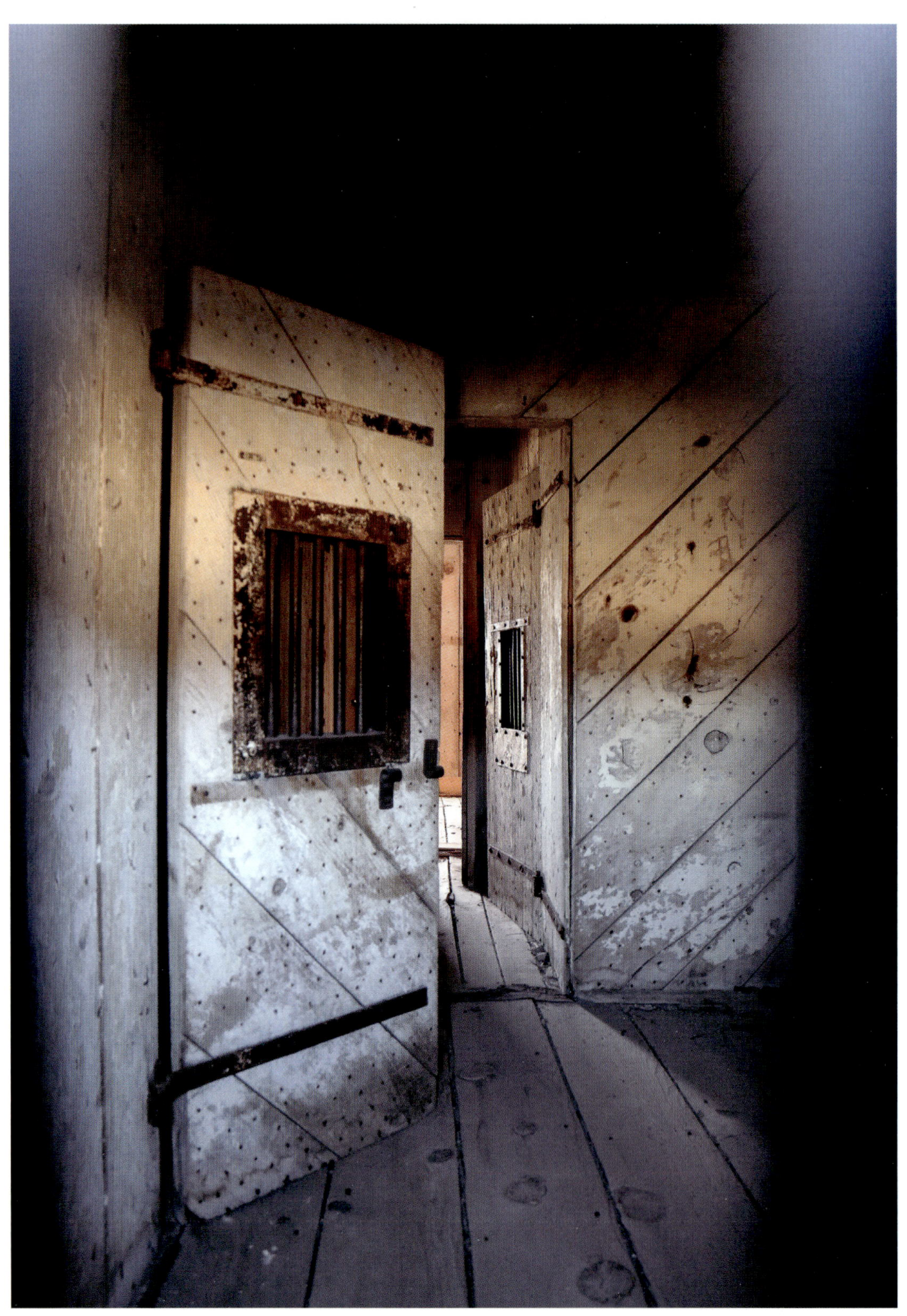

The heavy door of a jail cell as viewed through window bars.

The *San Francisco Argonaut* published a short story called "The Bad Man from Bodie," a fictional anecdote about a swaggering, boastful, violent man, which played upon the reputation Bodie residents had acquired in the outside world.

This wasn't the first or last paper to publish salacious stories about the booming mining town. The *San Francisco Daily Alta California* published an article describing Bodie thusly: "Saloons and gambling hells abound. There are at least sixty saloons in the place and not a single church." The *Saturday Evening Post* had the following to say, after interviewing a local for an article on September 25, 1915:

> In her feverish prime, Bodie boasted of the widest street in any Western mining camp, the wickedest men, and the worst climate out of doors.

The local population's mass flight outwards started in the mid-1880s, when prospectors became repeatedly disappointed with their excavations and realized they had most likely overestimated the amount of gold in the region. After reaching a peak population of around 8,000 people, stores and houses alike became rapidly abandoned. By 1915, the Standard Mine had closed and mining in the area had come to almost a complete halt—only around 200 people remained in town.

Some locals held out hope for a second gold rush in the area, especially when a multi-national corporation bought out and reopened a group of old mines in Bodie in 1929. This part of the town's history is represented by a couple of remaining abandoned cars of the era, as well as a sign for Shell gas, both items that would not have been around at the time of Bodie's peak years or initial founding.

However, a major gold deposit was never found in the area again, leading to Bodie's permanent abandonment. These days, Bodie is a State Park preserved in a condition of "arrested decay." It is widely considered one of the best-preserved Old West ghost towns in the entire United States, and has resisted the fate of other such places that have ended up as tourist traps and amusement parks.

When you enter Bodie today, you see dirt streets lined by plenty of remaining buildings, including saloons, hotels, a church, a barber shop, and several houses, preserved in their original state as much as possible. Clothes and items from the era are strewn inside the abodes; most are too unstable to allow visitors to enter, with only a couple of exceptions where you can take a look around.

Certain buildings, such as the local banks, are no longer standing; however, important parts of the structure, such as the safe and vault, remain intact. Other buildings give visitors a glimpse into how families in the Old West lived, with furniture from the original inhabitants remaining in the rooms, allowing visitors a peak into another era through the windows. Further on out from the main town, a couple of

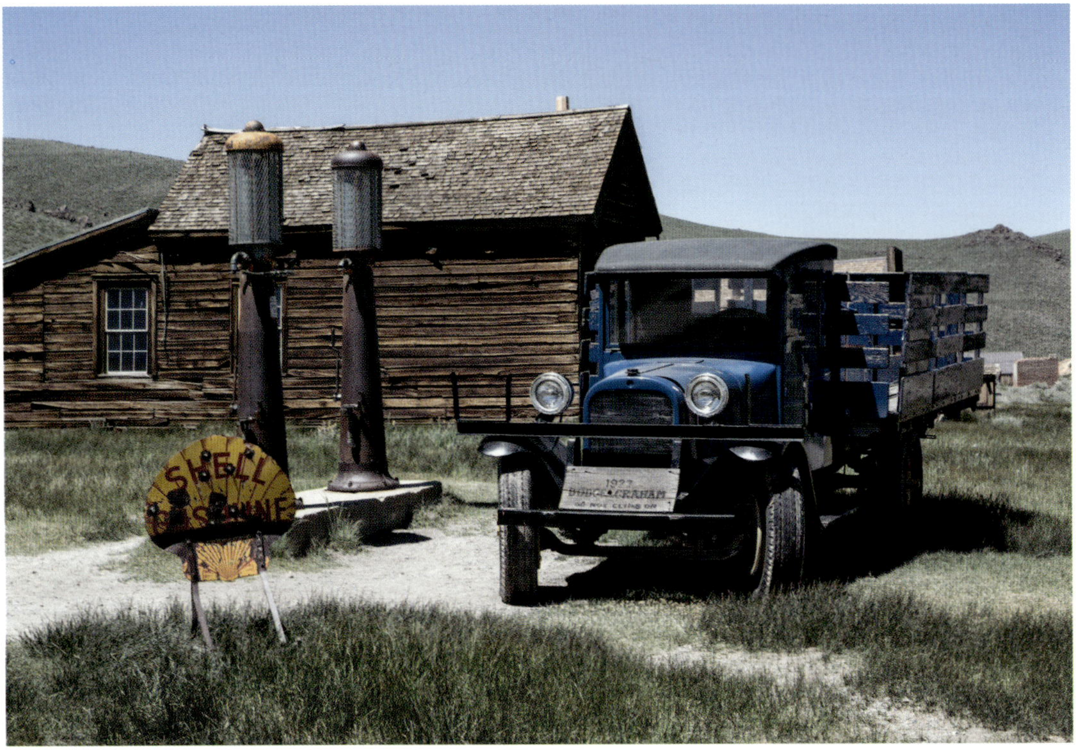

An old car and Shell gas sign from the latter days of Bodie.

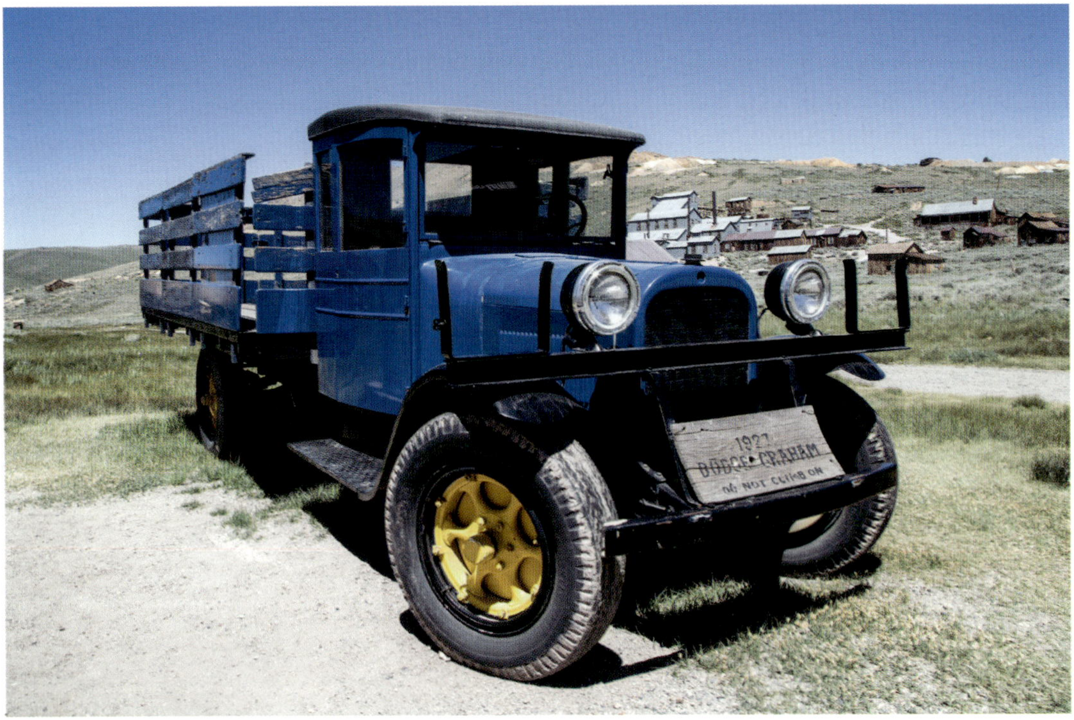

Close up of a classic blue car from the early twentieth century.

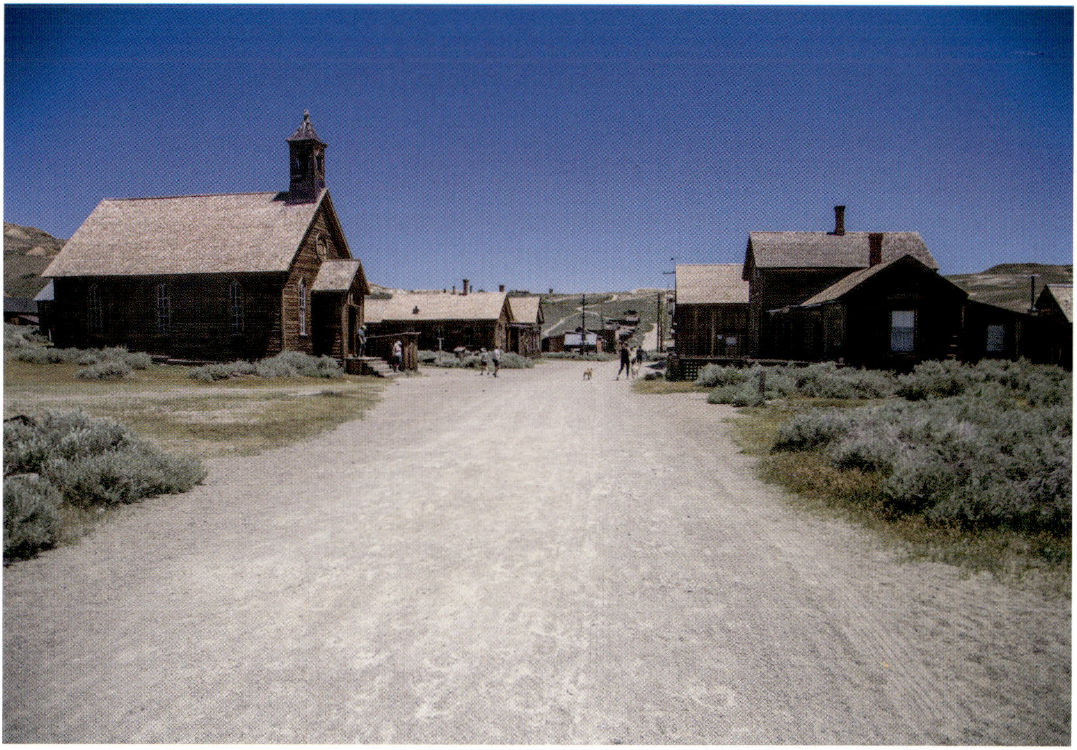

Walking into the town of Bodie on the main (dirt) road.

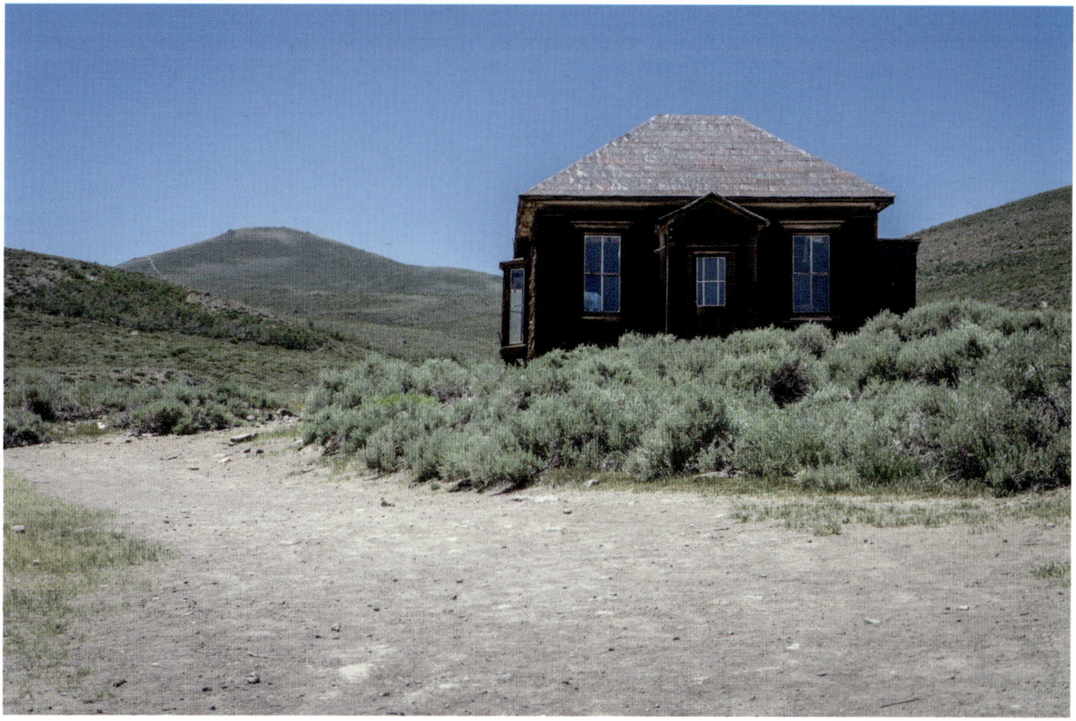

A lone house stands on the outskirts of Bodie.

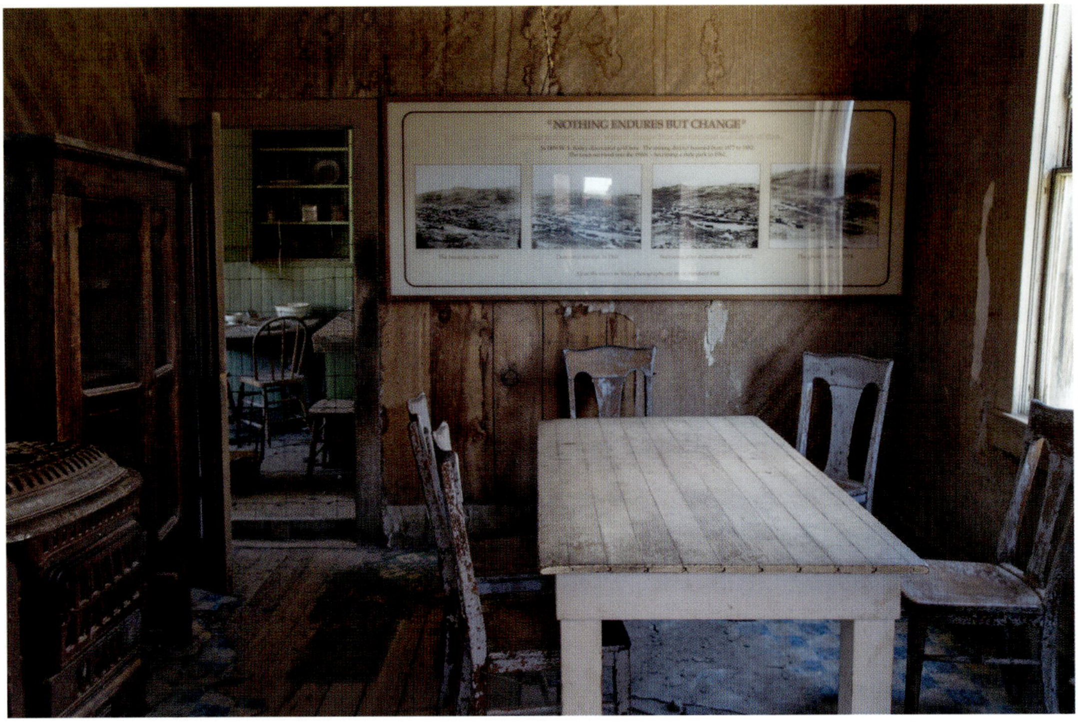

The common area of the only house in Bodie guests can enter.

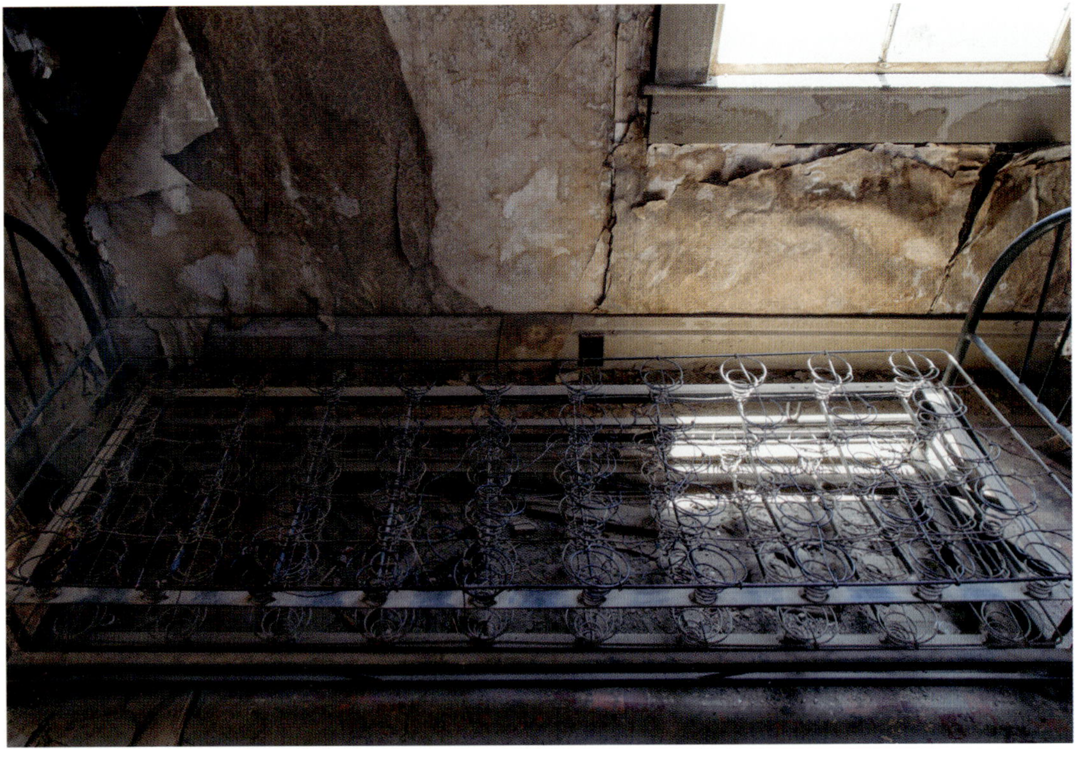

Only springs remain from what was once a bed in this house.

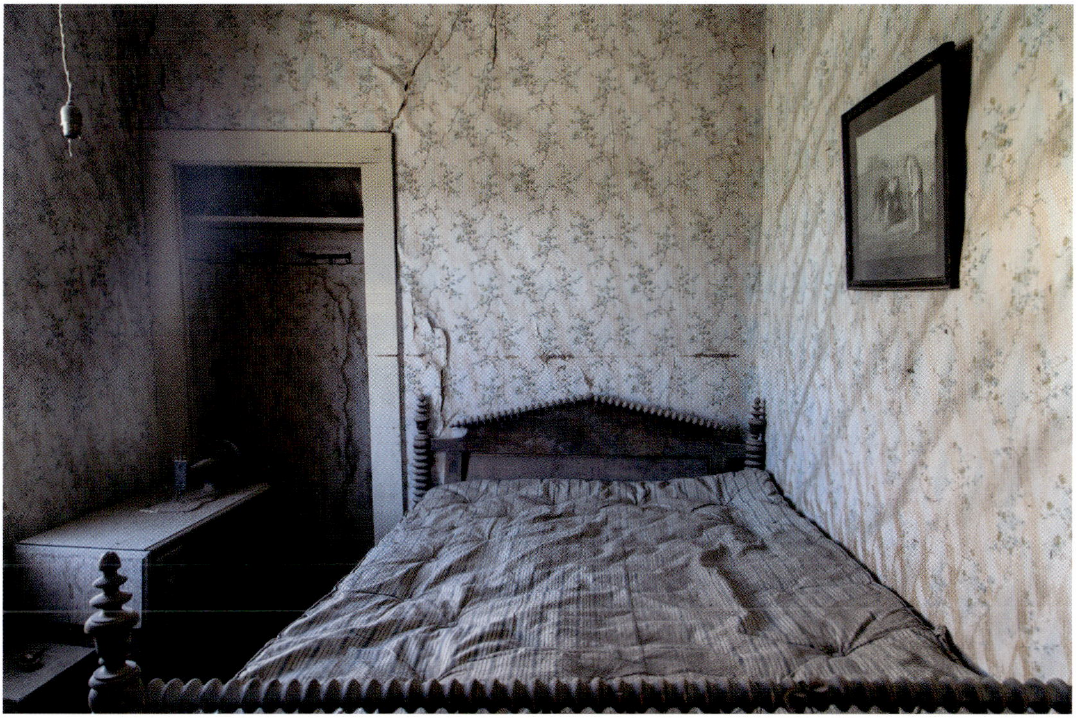

Light shines through a bedroom still decorated in the way it would have been back in Bodie's heyday.

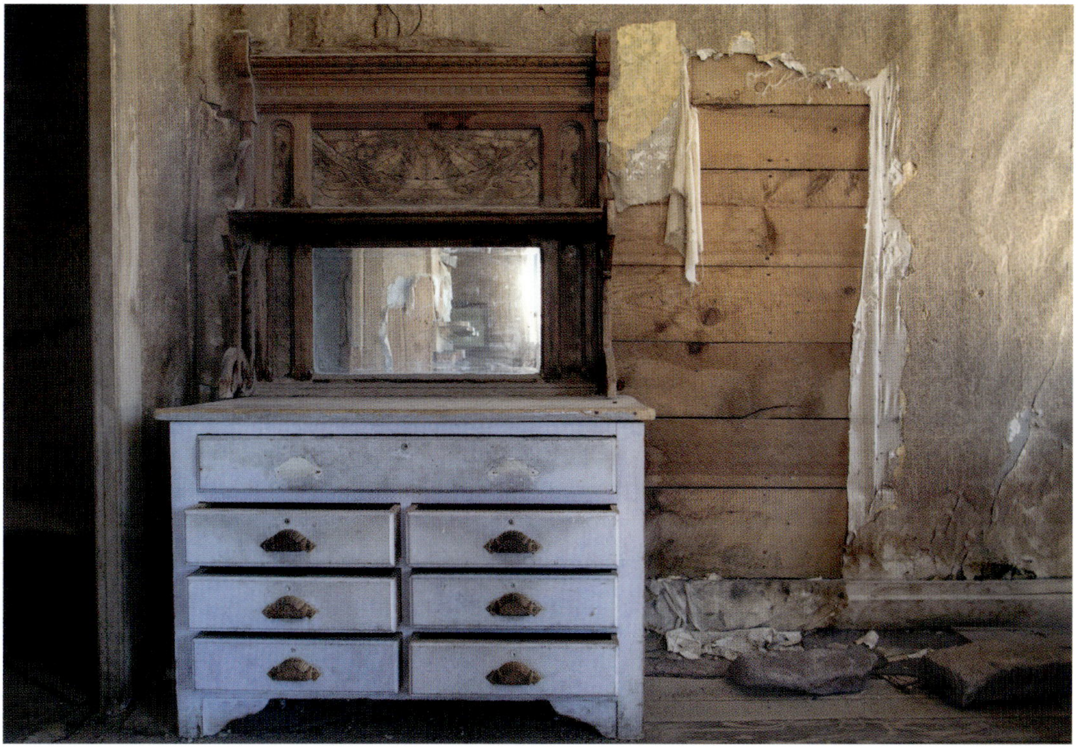

A dresser against a crumbling wall in a local home.

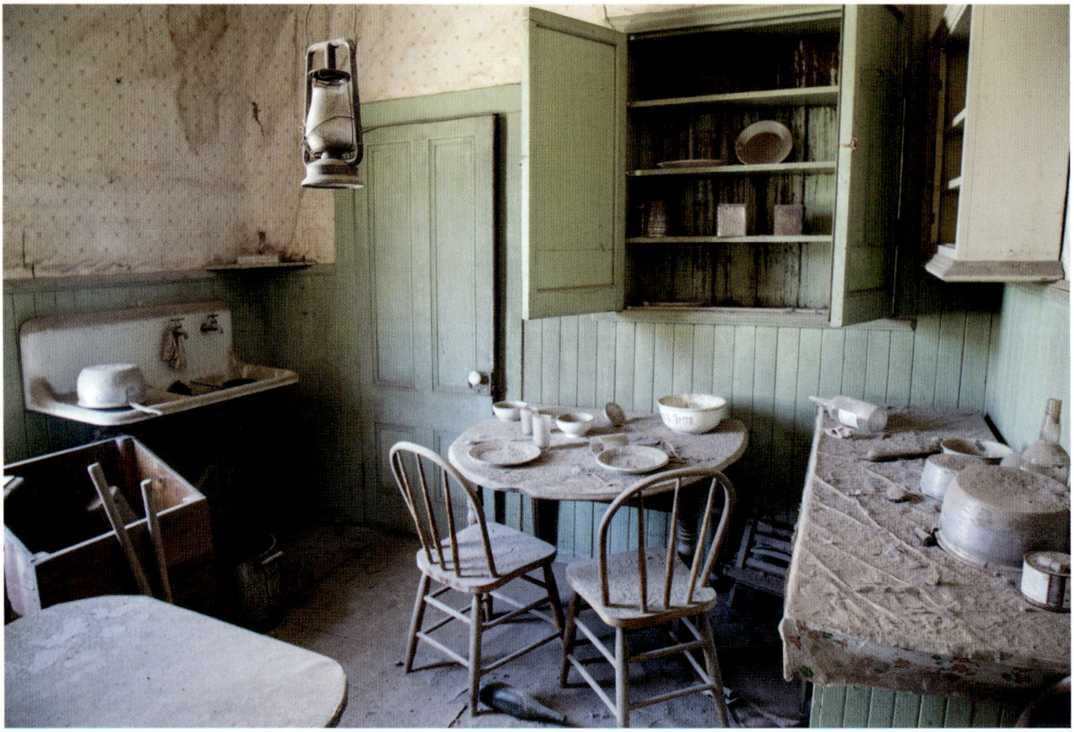

Looking into a dusty Old West kitchen.

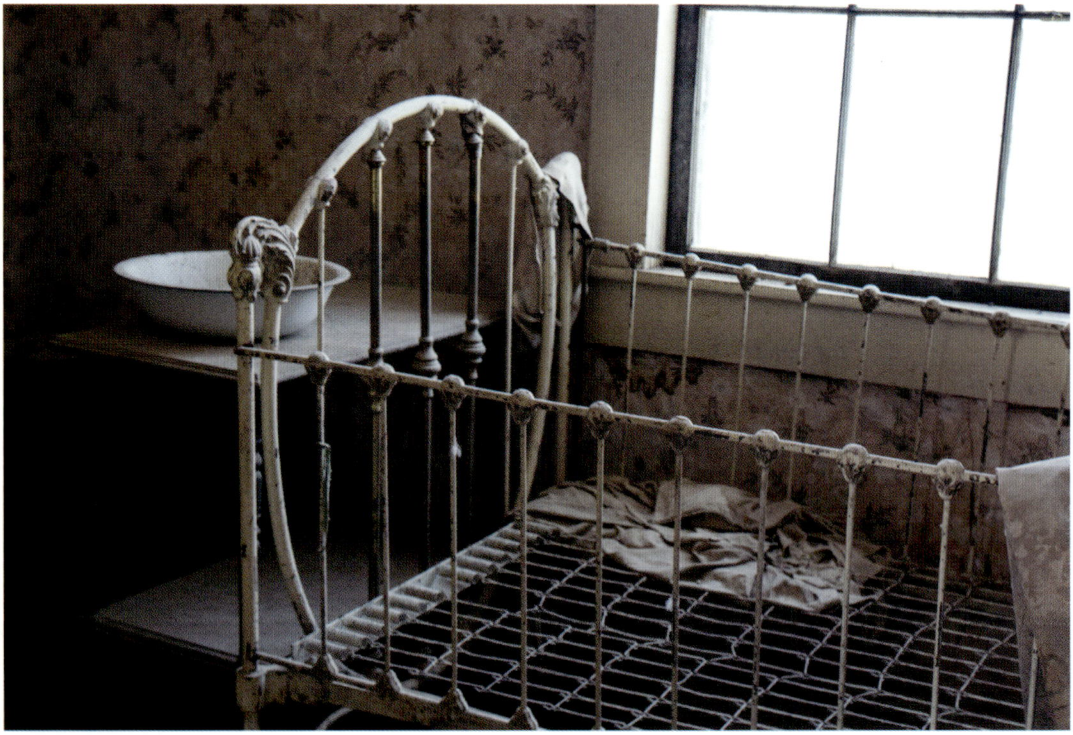

A small adjoining room in a Bodie home with a baby's crib.

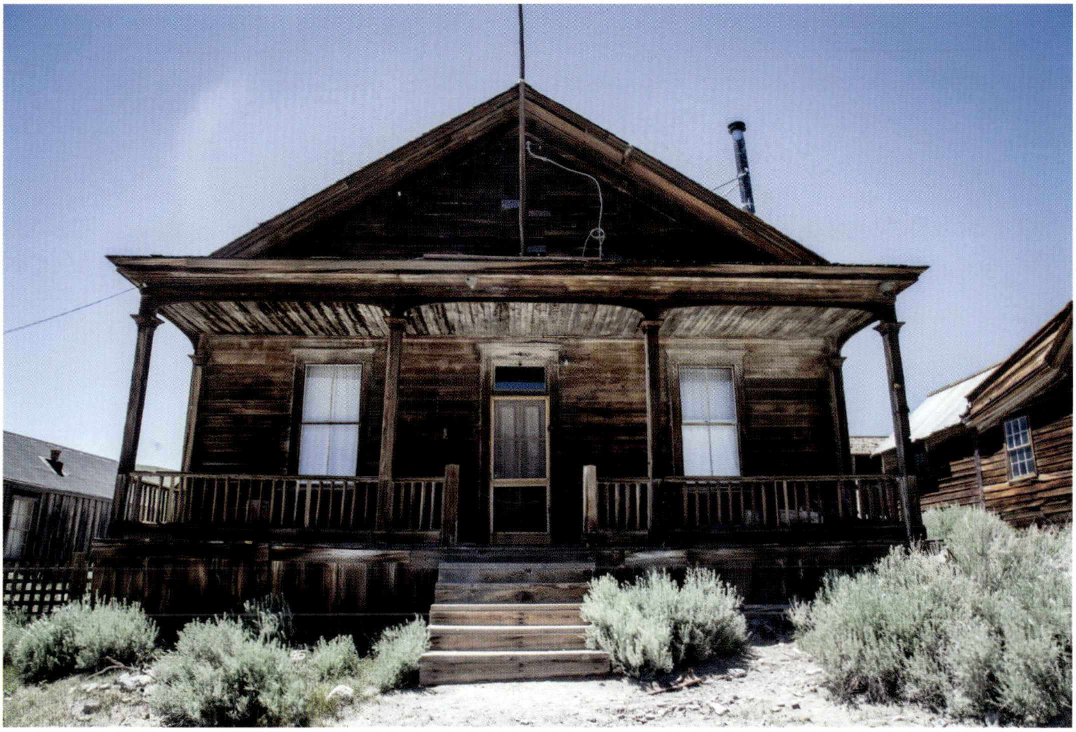

The façade of a well-off Bodie former resident's house.

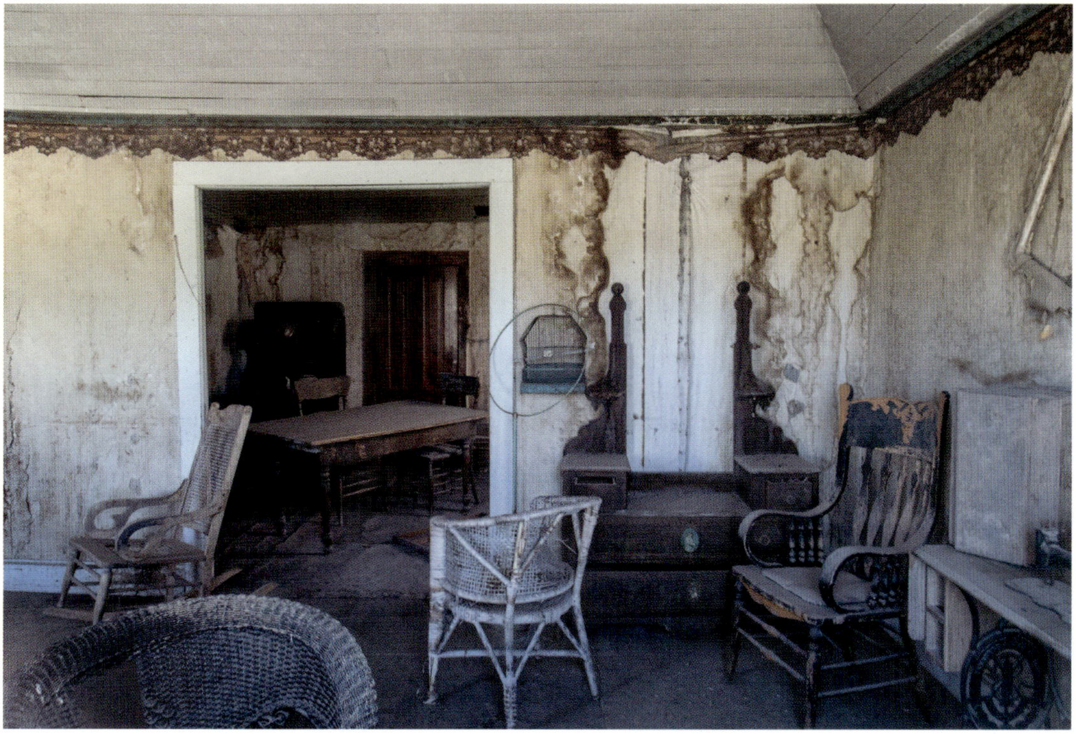

Water damage and long-term wear and tear is visible on the interior of this home.

structures from Bodie's Chinatown remain, including houses and a Chinese laundry, as the town boasted a significant Chinese minority.

The multiple hotels, entertainment halls, and supply stores still remaining give visitors an idea of how many people were flowing into Bodie at its peak, from other parts of the country and other parts of the world. Meanwhile, the school and church, two of the best-preserved buildings in the town, show the more lawful, peaceful turn Bodie took after the start of its decline.

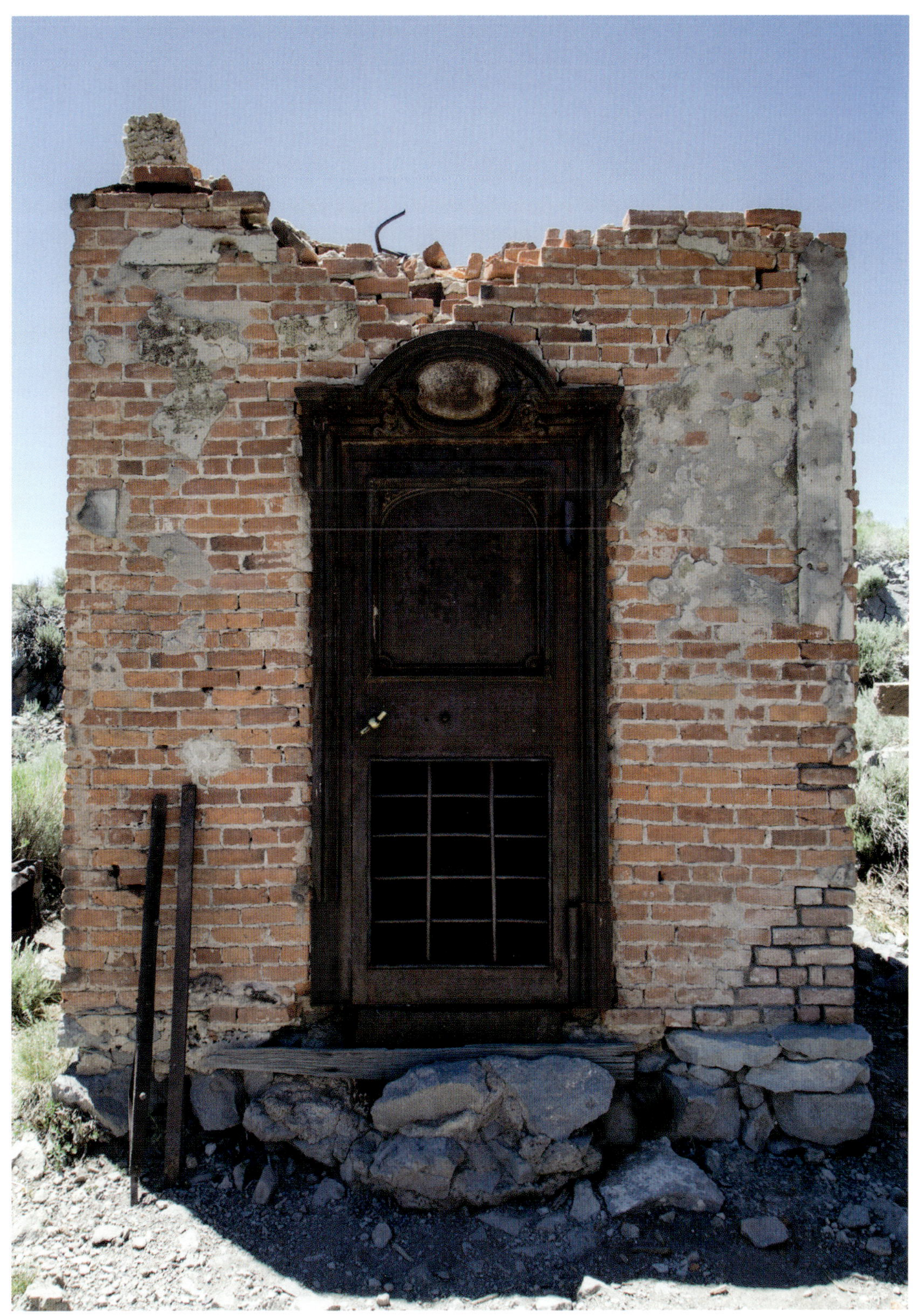

The only part of the bank that remains.

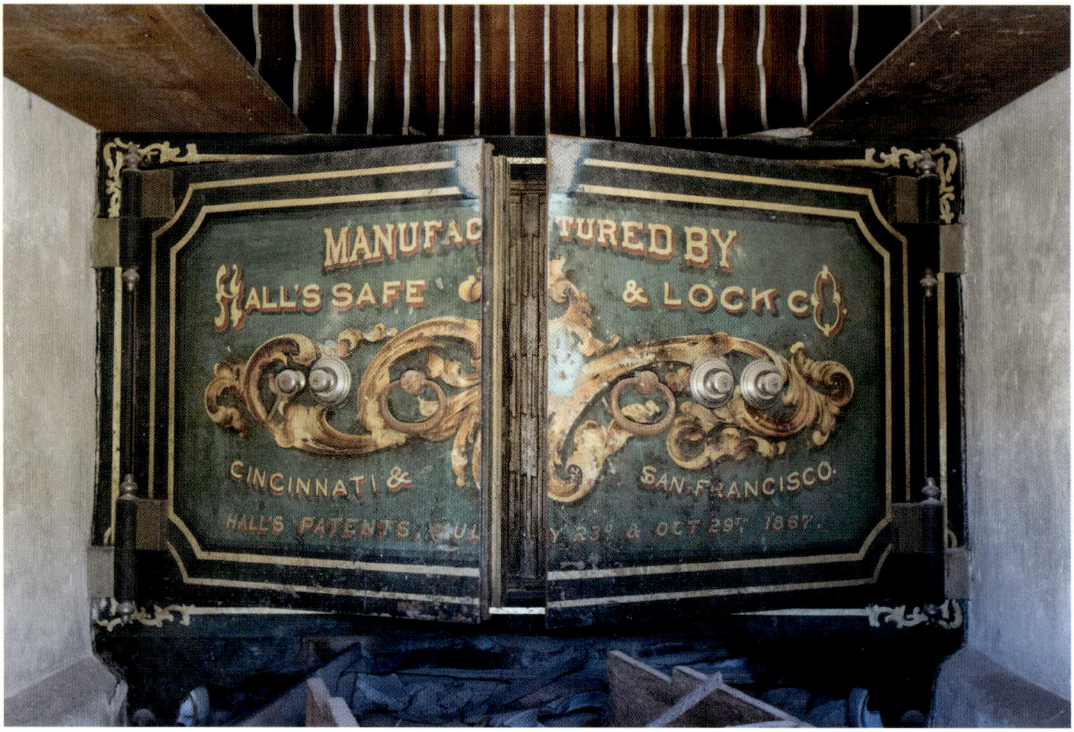

All that's left of the local Bodie bank is the brightly decorated safe.

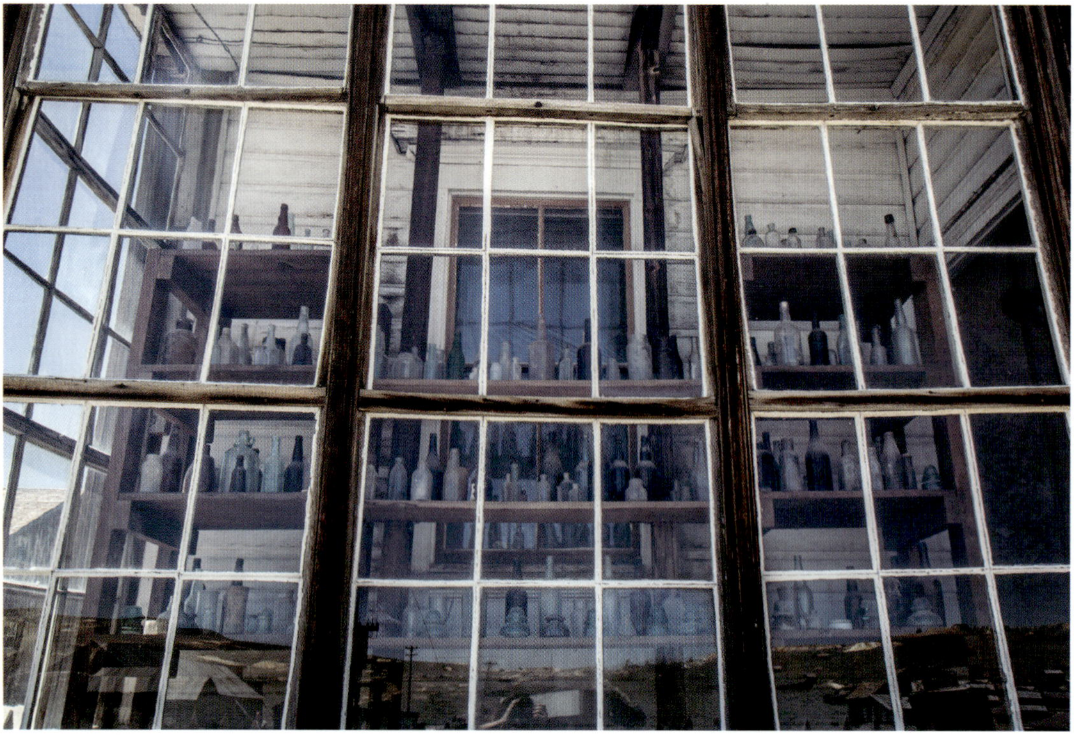

The window and wares of Bodie's general store.

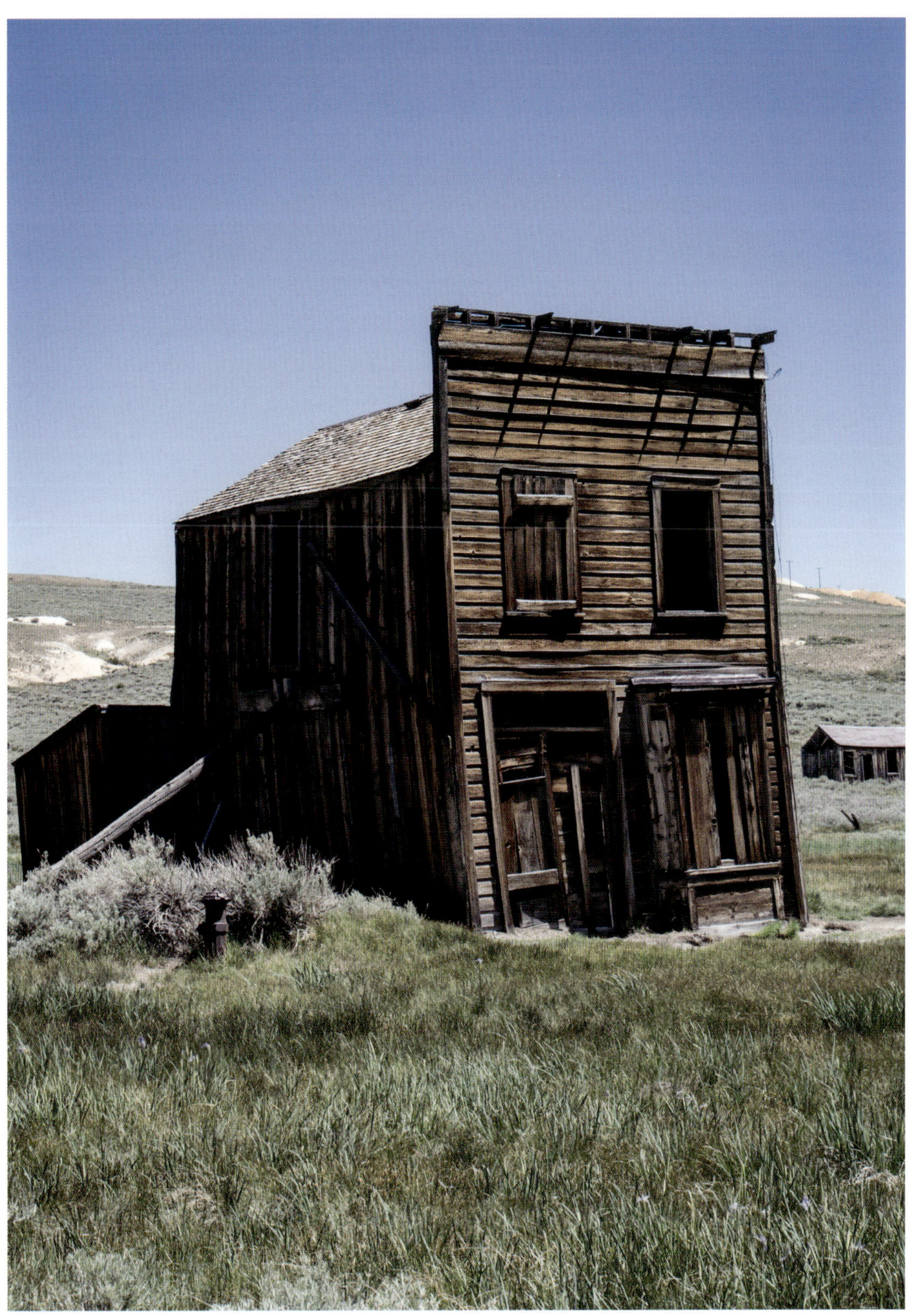

A former Bodie hotel, now leaning towards collapse.

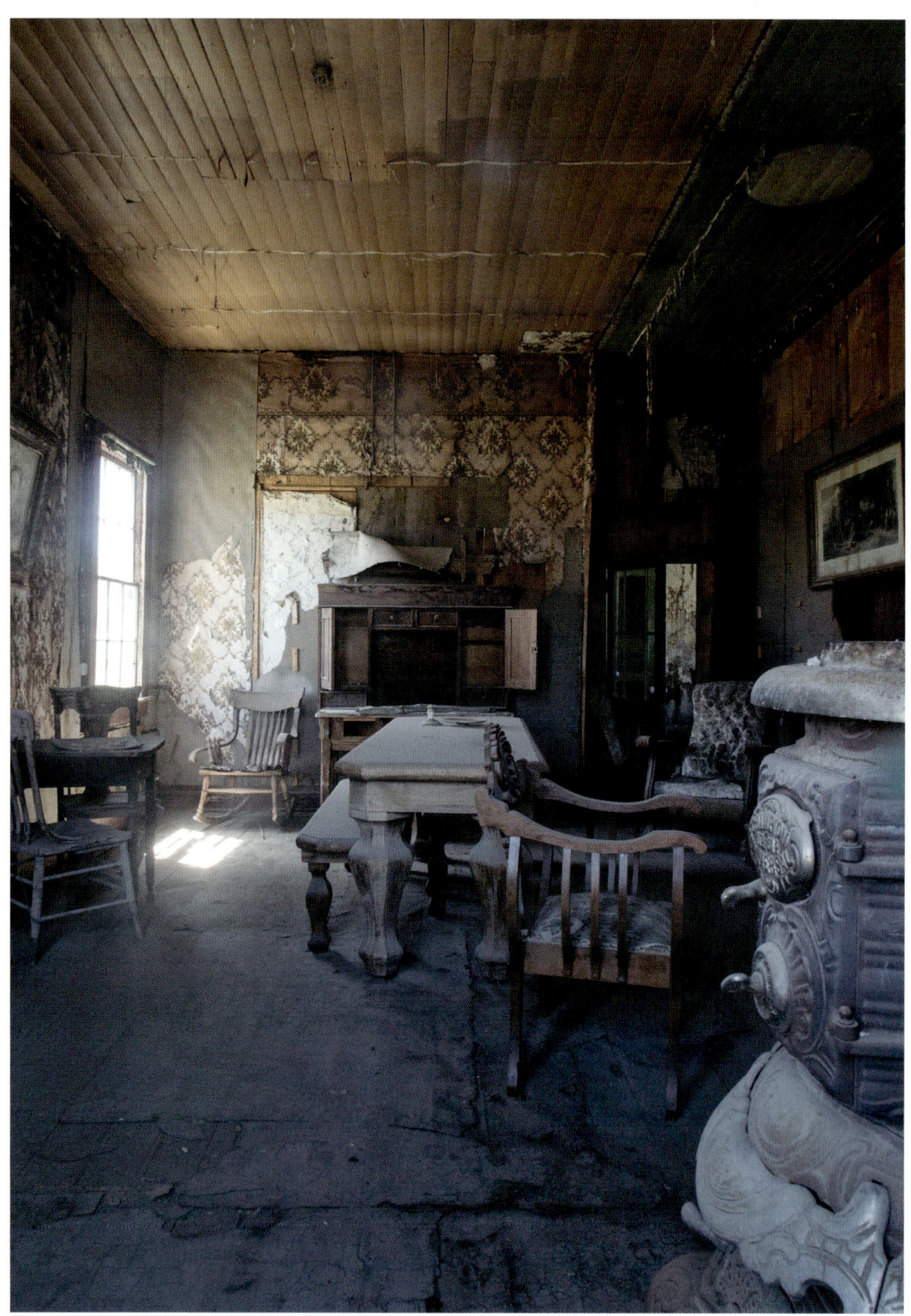

Upscale interior furnishings decaying in a home.

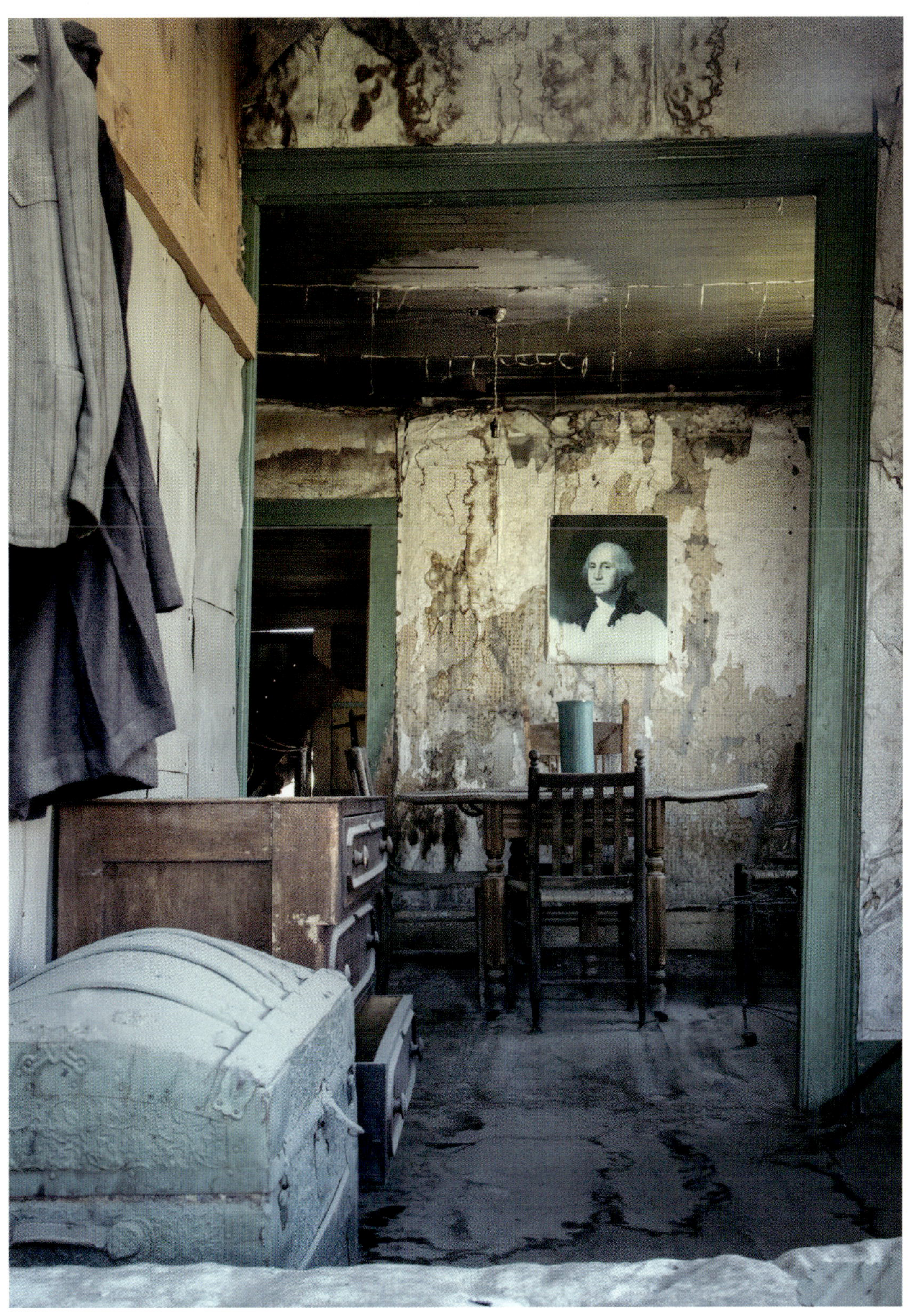

A portrait of George Washington hangs in the background.

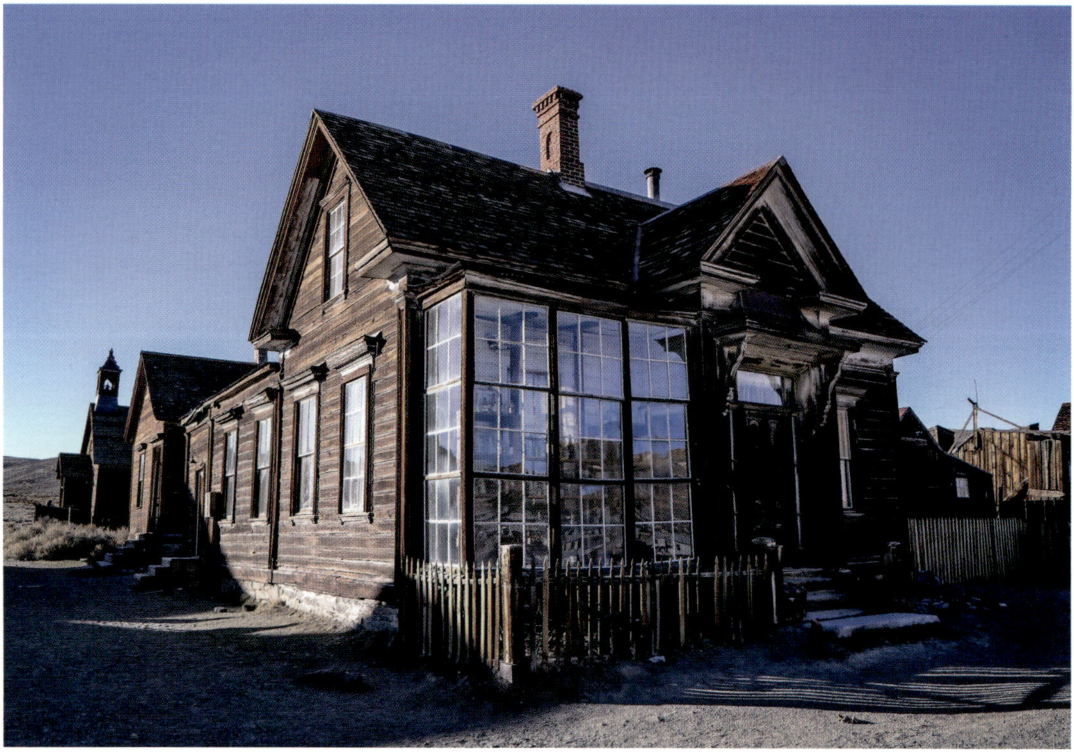

The Bodie General store on the town's main road.

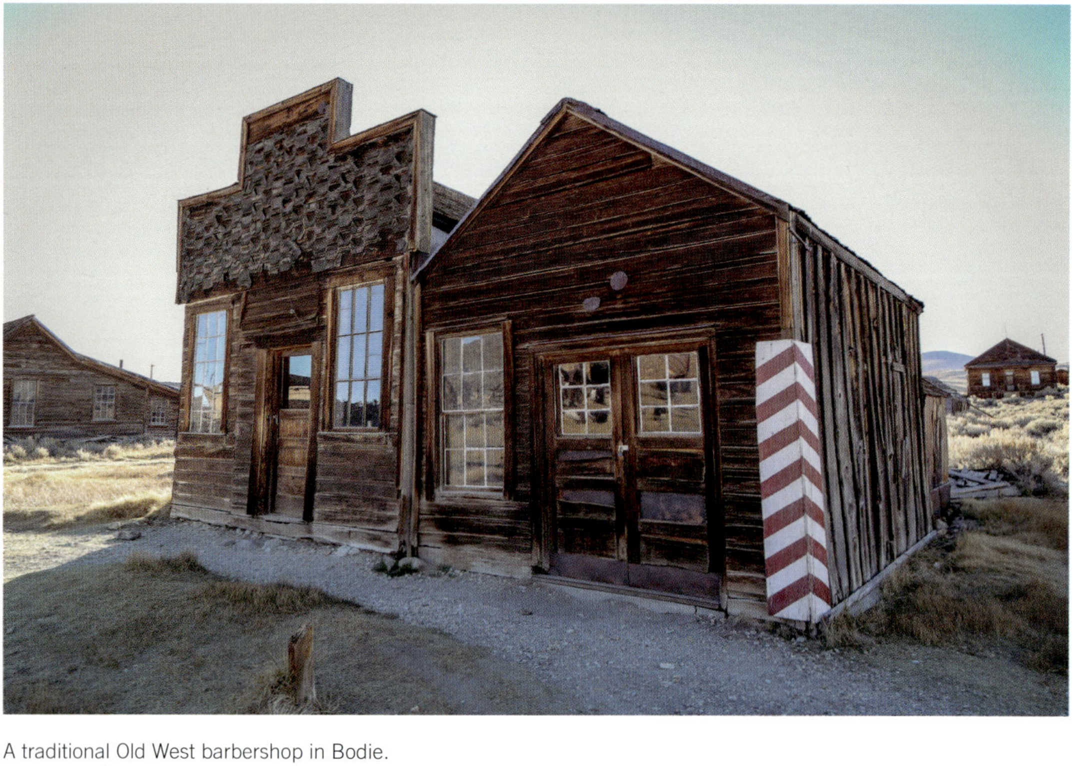

A traditional Old West barbershop in Bodie.

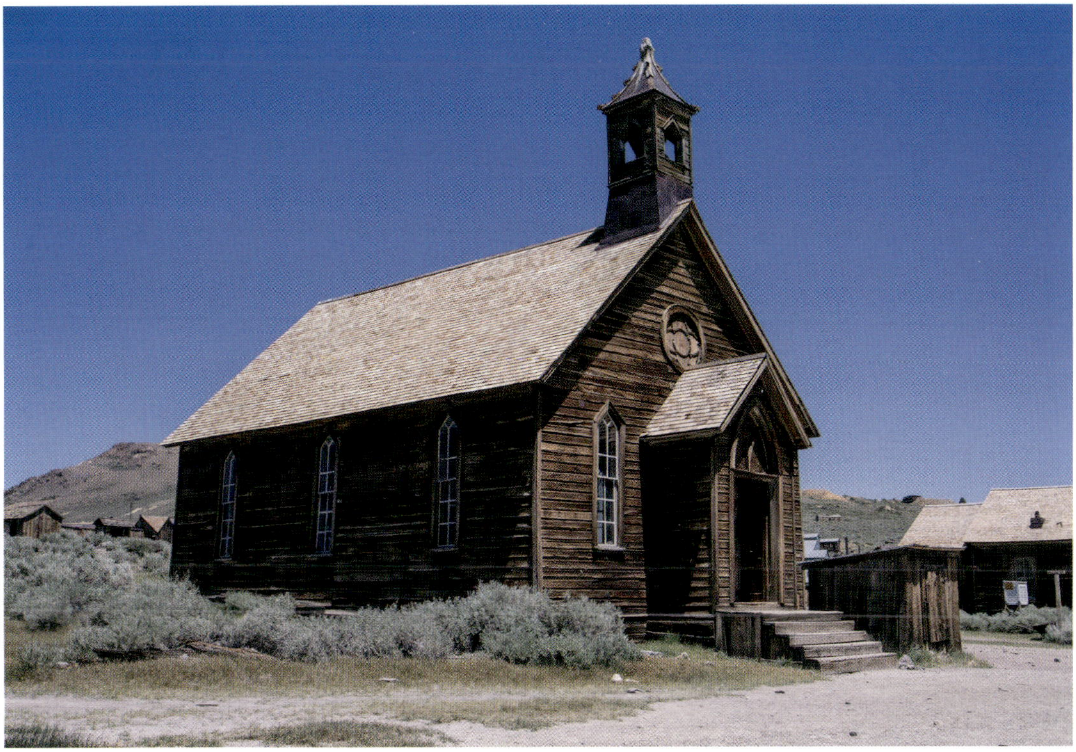

A side view of Bodie's church, one of the best-preserved buildings in the town.

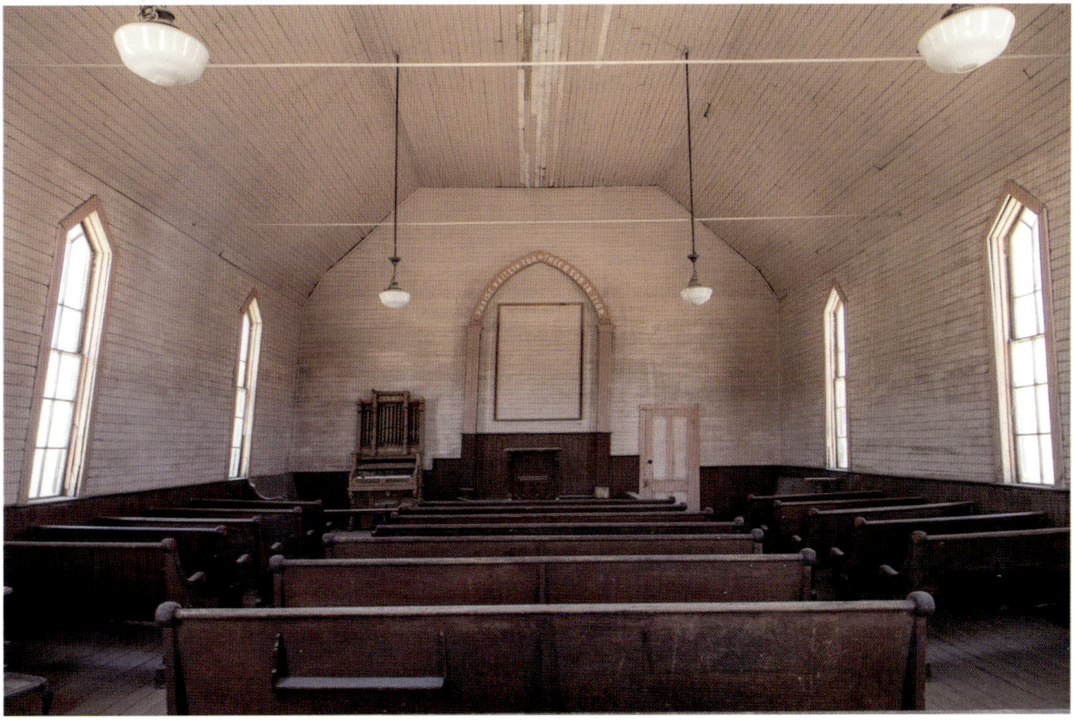

The interior of Bodie's church; the pews and seats are still preserved.

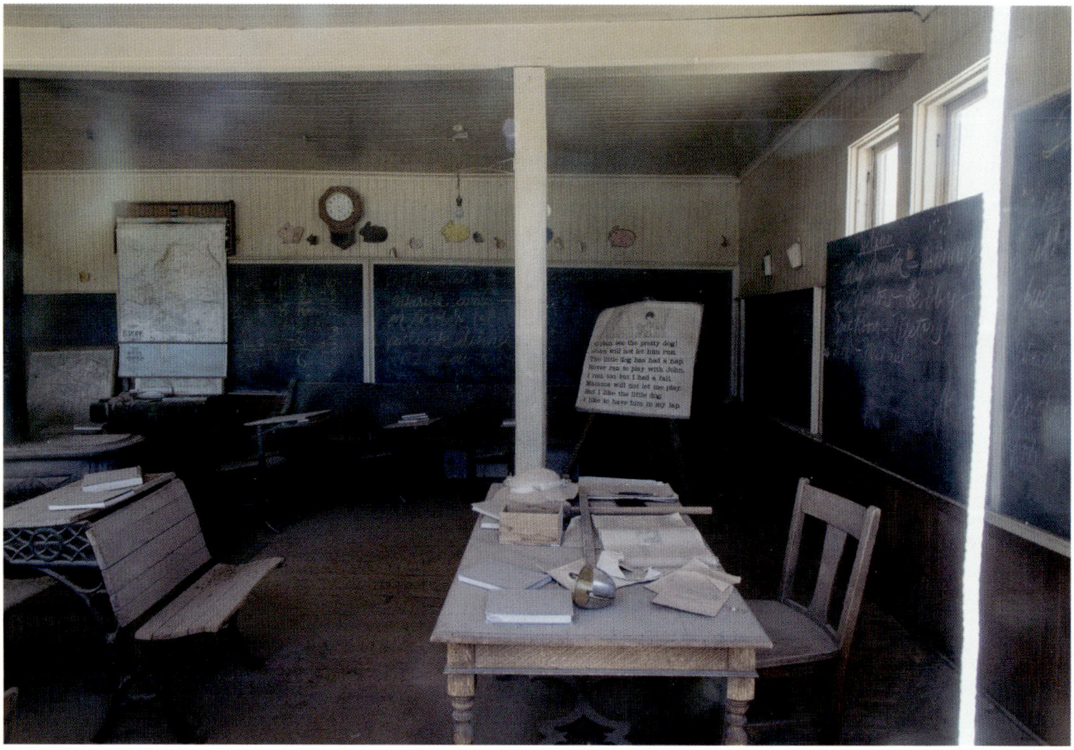

The teacher's desk and blackboard in the old Bodie school.

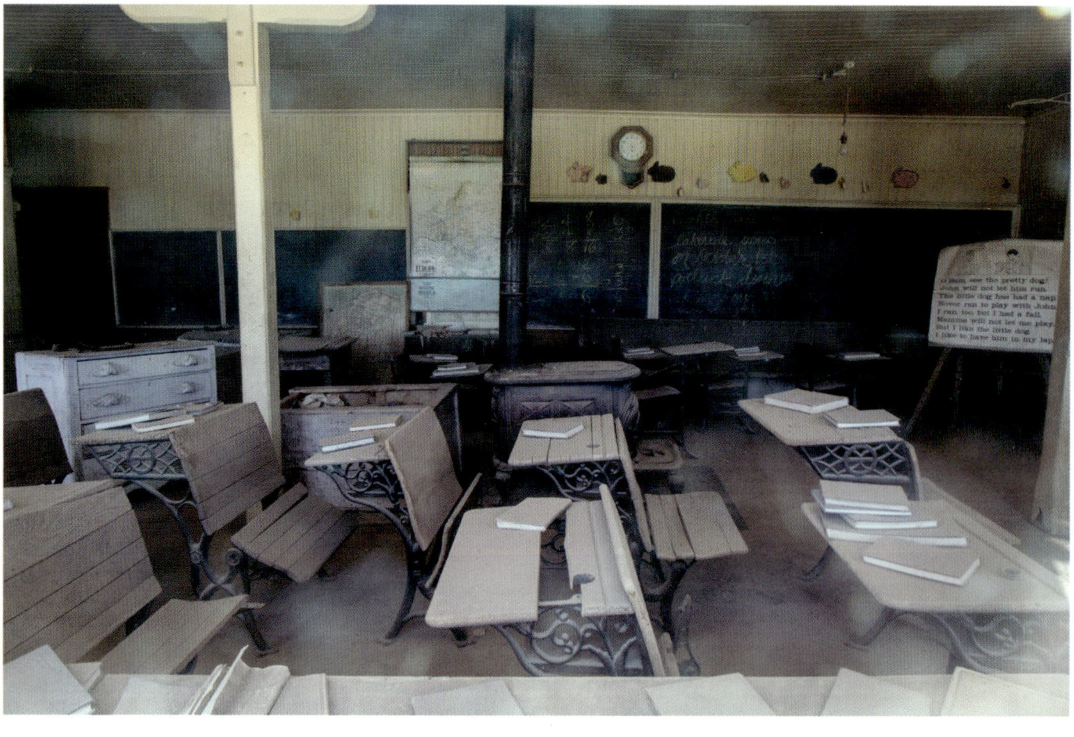

Another view of the school interior.

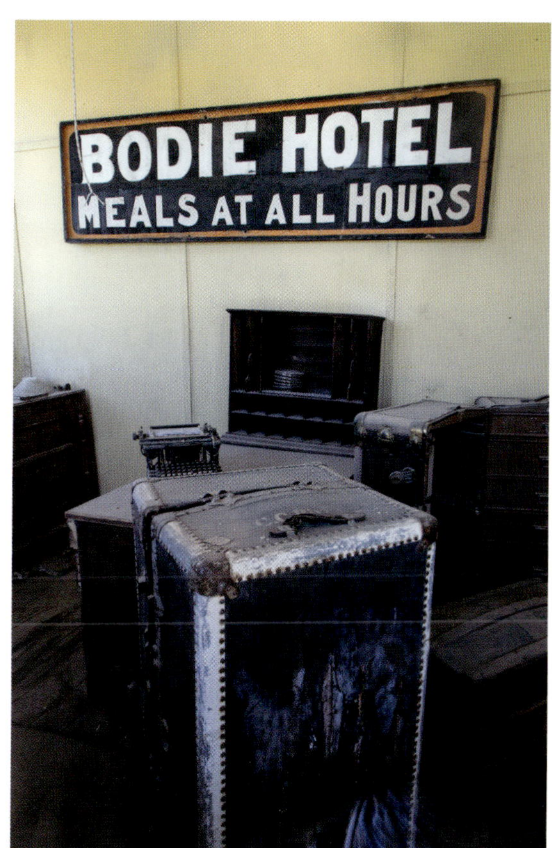

Right: Left-behind luggage in the entrance hall of a Bodie hotel.

Below: Basic items and daily necessities of the Old West in the general store.

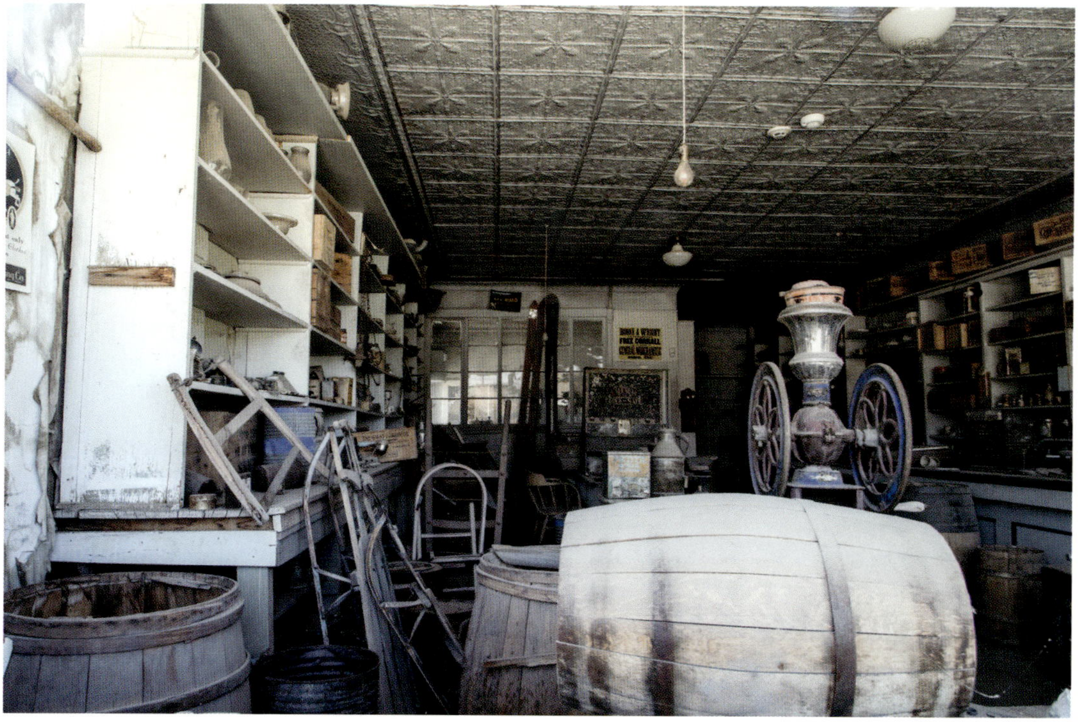

2

THE RAILROAD HEADS WEST

The engineers and workers who laid down railroad tracks through the rocky, cold mountains and endless forests of central and northern California had no easy task to accomplish. The weather in the area fluctuates between wild extremes during the year, the landscape is daunting and challenging, and the sheer elevation of the mountains and cliff drops present in some locations can make constructing a railroad difficult, to say the least.

Built mostly by Chinese immigrants, who often died in the process of constructing tunnels using dangerously inaccurate techniques of the time involving nitroglycerin and dynamite, the railroad was one of the most important developments for the creation of the West as we know it today. This revolutionary development cut down travel times from East Coast to West Coast to just under a week, bringing an enormous influx of immigrants from the East to California. Compared to the rapidly increasing and crowded conditions of East Coast cities, California was seen as a promised land both for US citizens tired of dense urban populations and diseases, and European immigrants who had initially landed in New York, only to find their new reality worse (and poorer) than expected.

It is almost impossible to impress the importance of the railroad to people in the Old West upon modern audiences, but perhaps an excerpt from the *Rocky Mountain News* in 1886 can summarize its significance:

> The one moral, the one remedy for every evil, social, political, financial, and industrial, the one immediate vital need of the entire Republic, is the Pacific Railroad.

The abandoned remains of the original railroad line give some insight into the harsh terrain these powerful trains had to cross on the journey out West, and the difficulty and danger involved in constructing these lines. No such ruins are more impressive than the abandoned tunnels of the Donner Pass.

DONNER PASS SUMMIT TUNNELS

The Donner Pass tunnels were constructed in 1867 to allow the Central Pacific Railroad access through the Sierra Nevada Mountains onto the city of Oakland, the last stop of its transcontinental journey. Built mostly by Chinese laborers, trains used the tunnels for just over 125 years, until 1993 when a new route was constructed through Mount Judah.

This part of the railroad journey was one of the most treacherous in the entire country. In fact, the Donner Pass was named after the infamous Donner Party tragedy, when explorers who became stranded in the unforgiving mountains engaged in cannibalism to survive the harsh, wintery conditions. This tragedy was a disturbing consequence of the dangerous and inhospitable conditions of the area.

On the informal hike up to the now abandoned tunnels, visitors can spot petroglyphs from California's original Native American population on the surrounding rocks. Further up, three tunnels remain: two short transitional tunnels, and one long, dark tunnel hewn into the rock, covered in graffiti, that seems to go on for miles. Light only enters through occasional slits into this endless passage, lending the tunnel an eerie quality.

THE STRANGE STORY OF THE 16TH STREET STATION

The railroad took a different, more elegant form in the cities it conquered. In the middle of a somewhat neglected part of Oakland lies the abandoned, yet stylishly designed 16th Street Station, looking somewhat incongruous against the backdrop of small, decaying houses in the neighborhood.

Just as the Donner Pass Summit Tunnels represent the roughest parts of the Pacific Railroad construction, the abandoned Oakland station represents the luxury and elegance associated with the actual railroad journey, especially in comparison to earlier methods of transport out West (including wagons and horseback). The original station was a simple wooden structure, but it was then replaced in 1912 by the Beaux-Arts building that stands there today.

The station's significance declined along with the general decline in rail use in the second half of the twentieth century. Amtrak took over the station in 1971, but service

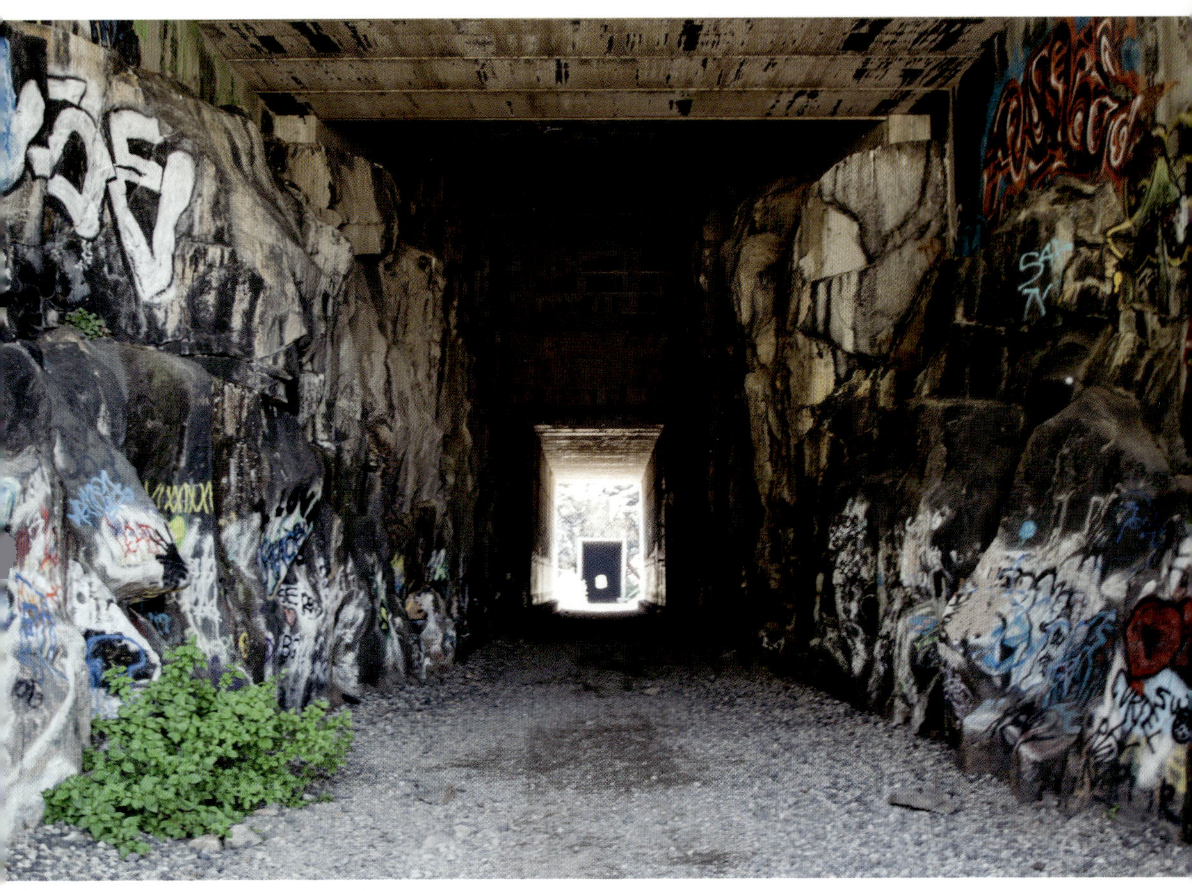

One of the shorter Donner Pass Summit Tunnels.

to the station eventually ended in 1994, partly due to the construction of Interstate 880, which forced the railroad tracks to be moved west. A major earthquake in 1989 that structurally damaged the building also probably influenced the decision to shut 16th Street Station down.

Though the station is technically currently abandoned, it has been taken over by a local redevelopment project intent on putting the beautifully constructed building to good use. The 16th Street Station is now home to several artistic and cultural events a year, and can also be rented for private events. It has also been used in movies and music videos, including Mumford & Sons' "Babel" video and *RENT*.

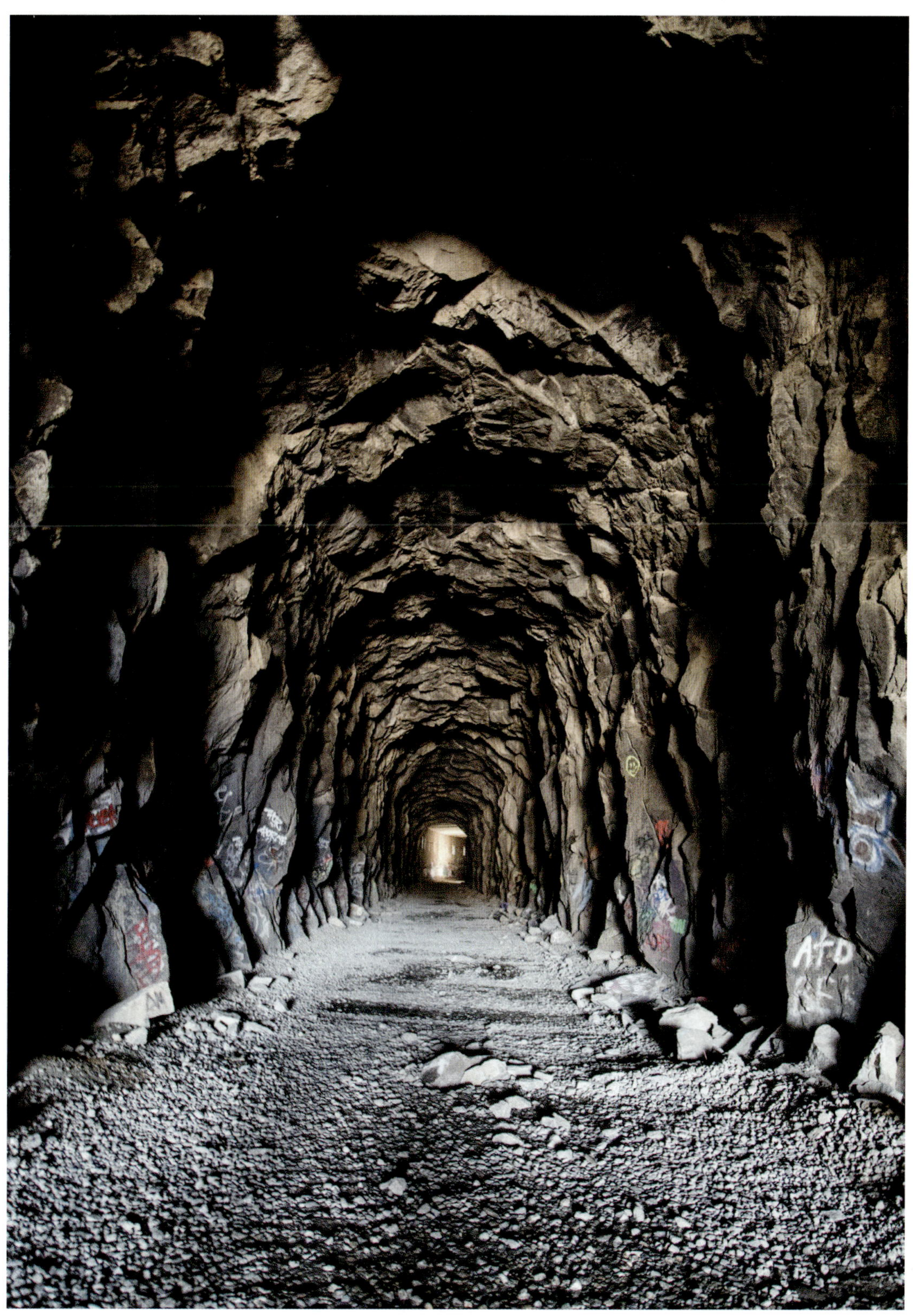

The longest tunnel of the Donner Pass Summit Tunnels, hewn into the rock of the mountain.

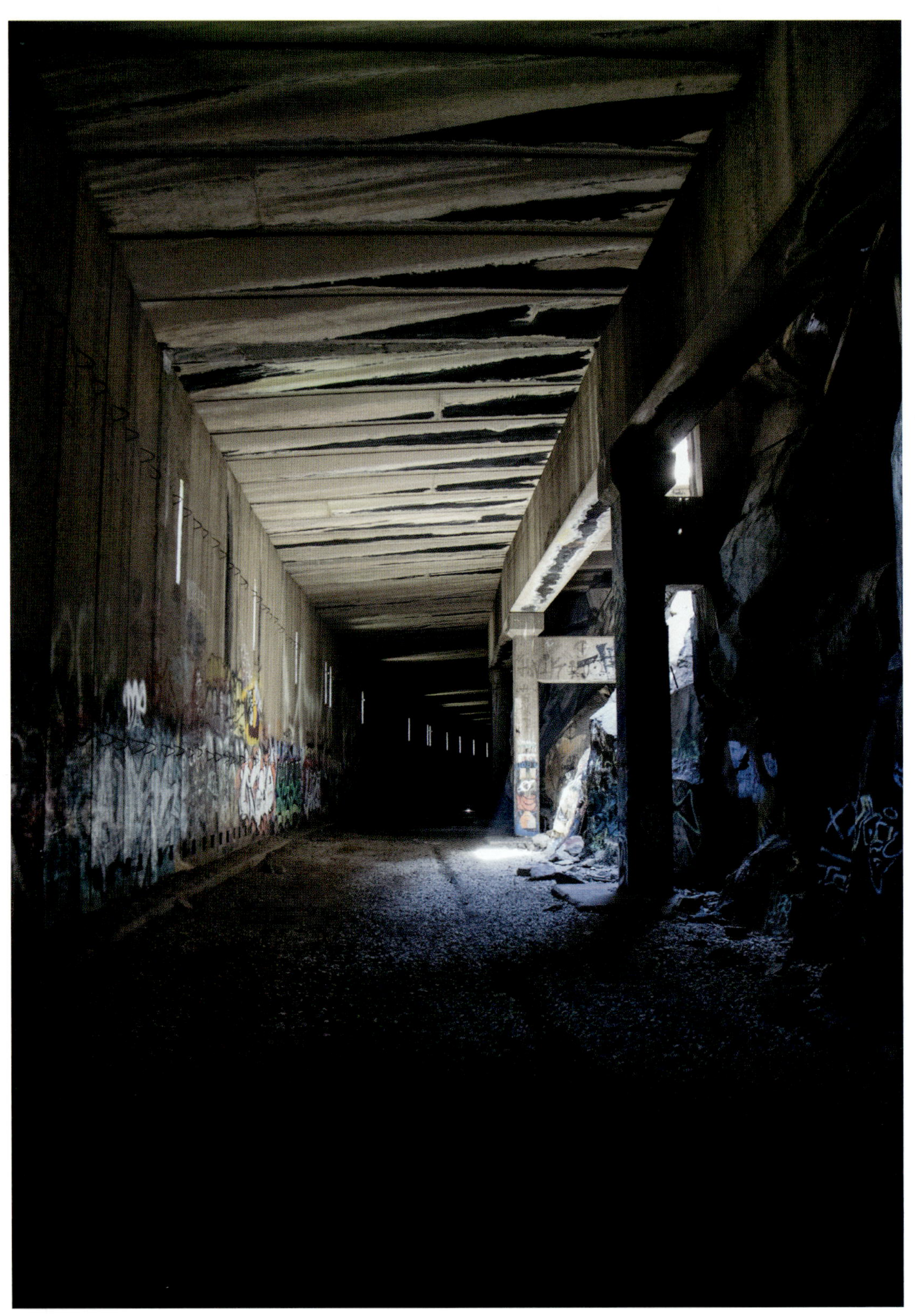

Light seeps through one of the few bright spots in the longest tunnel.

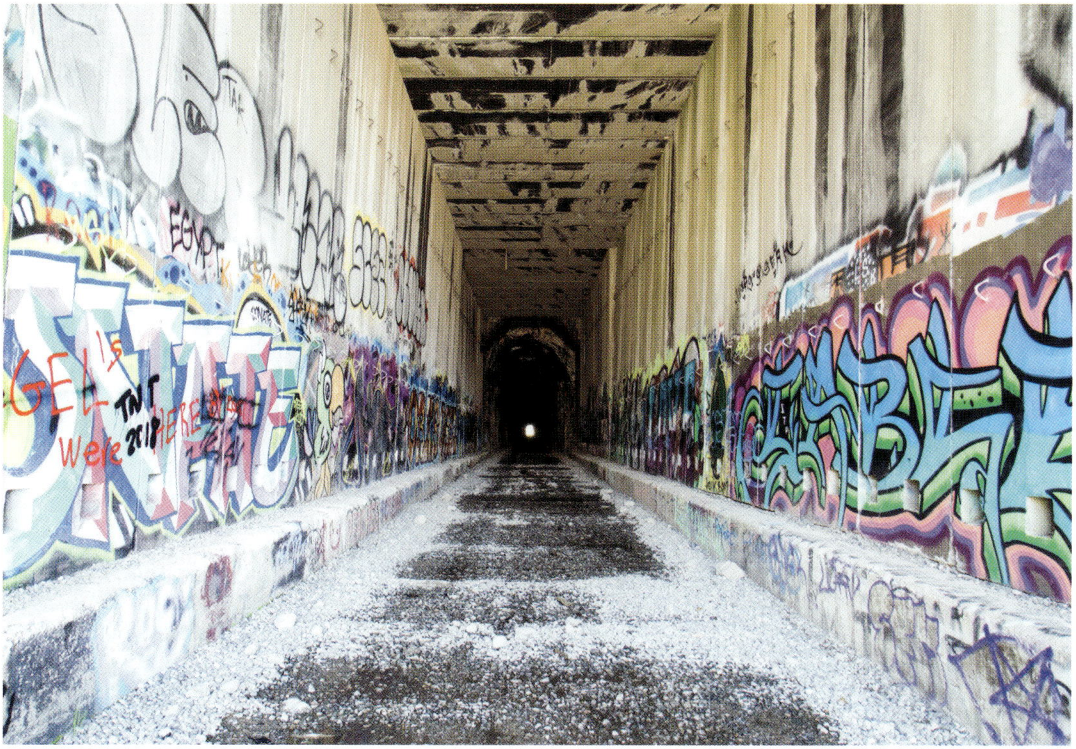

More street art in the tunnels; the tunnel system is covered in graffiti.

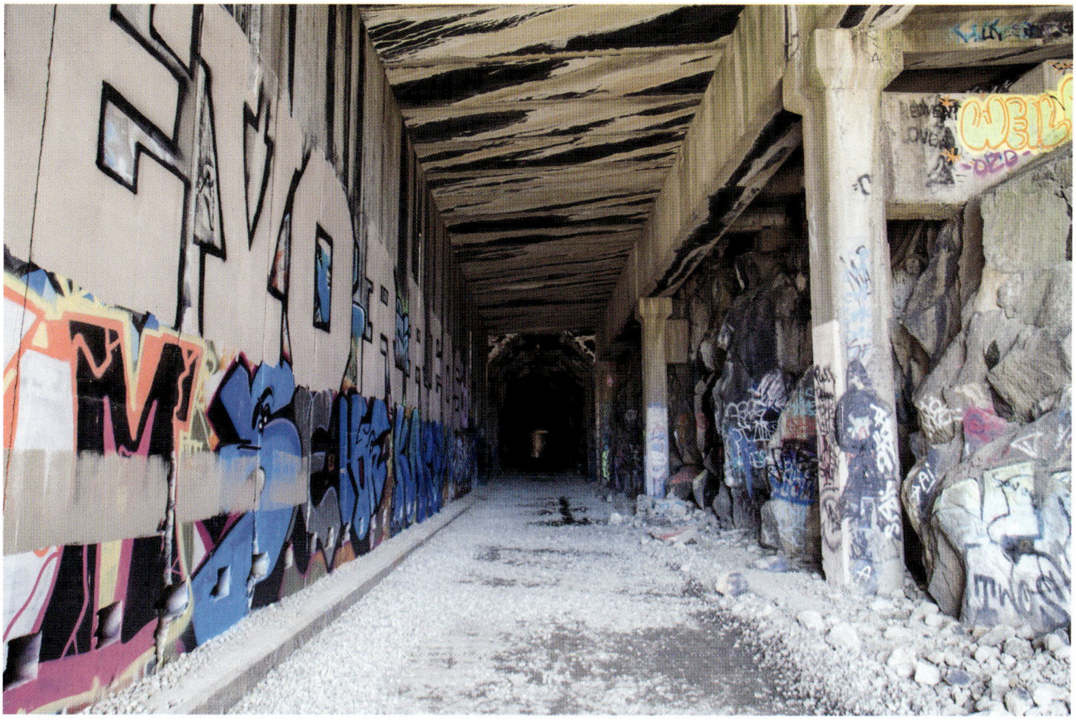

The tunnel for the old railroad is clearly visible.

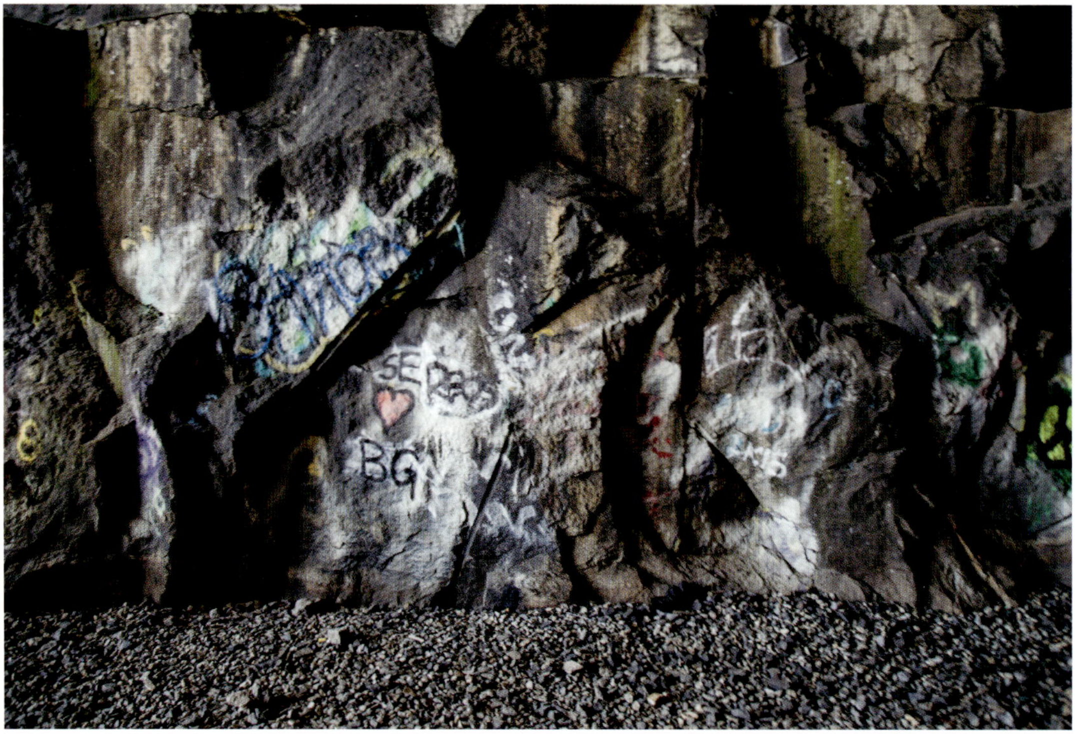

Graffiti in the tunnels.

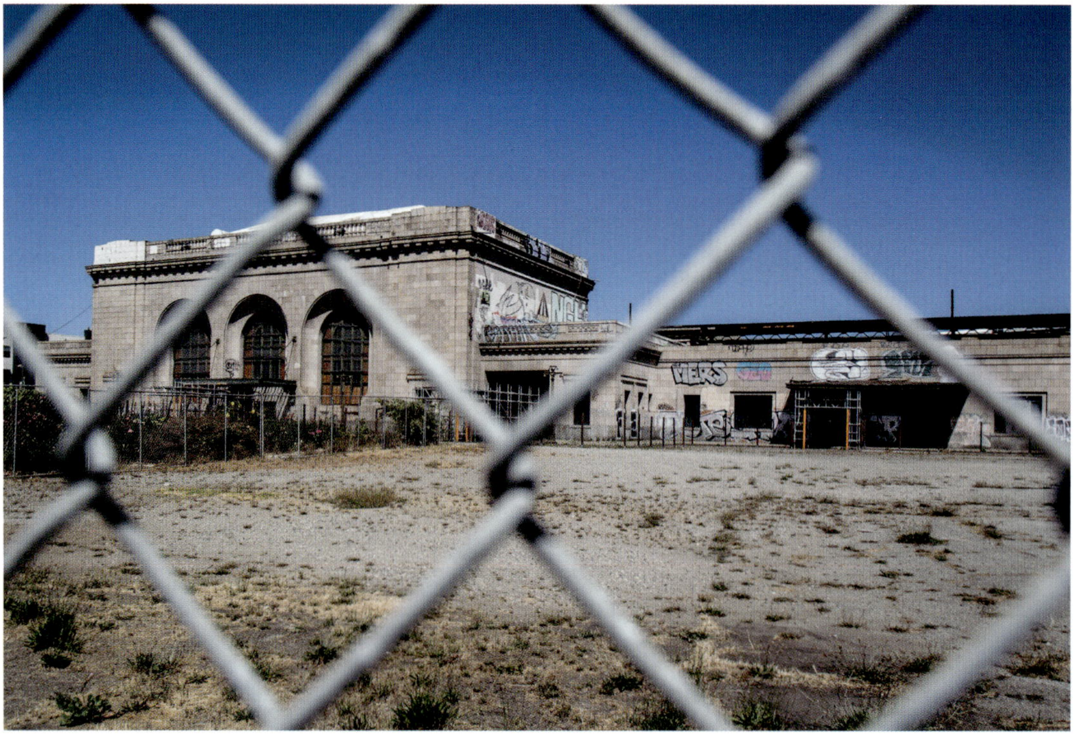

Looking at 16th Street Station in Oakland through a chain link fence.

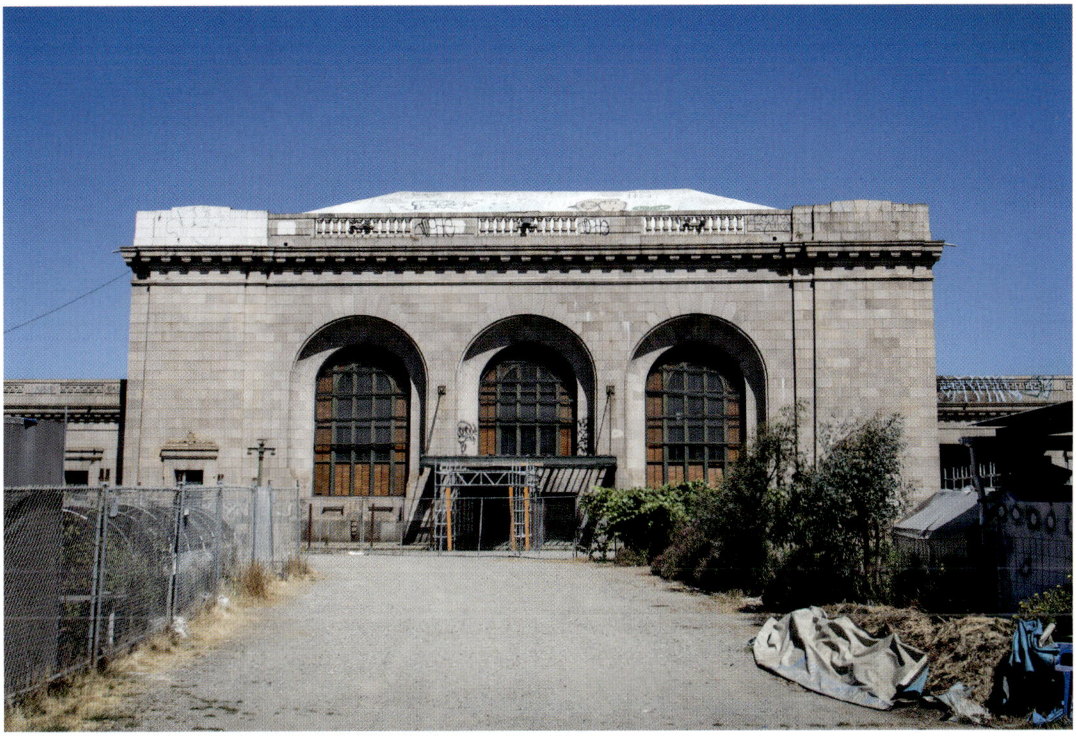

The Beaux-Arts building still retains its old elegance.

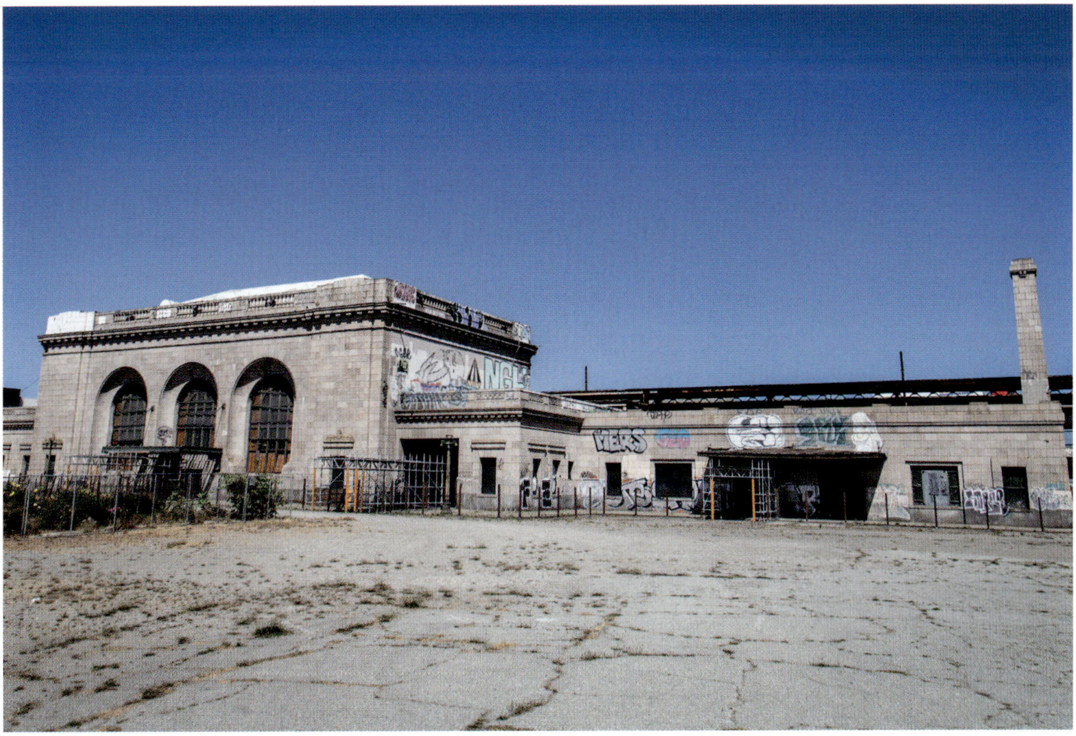

Another view of the abandoned rail station in Oakland.

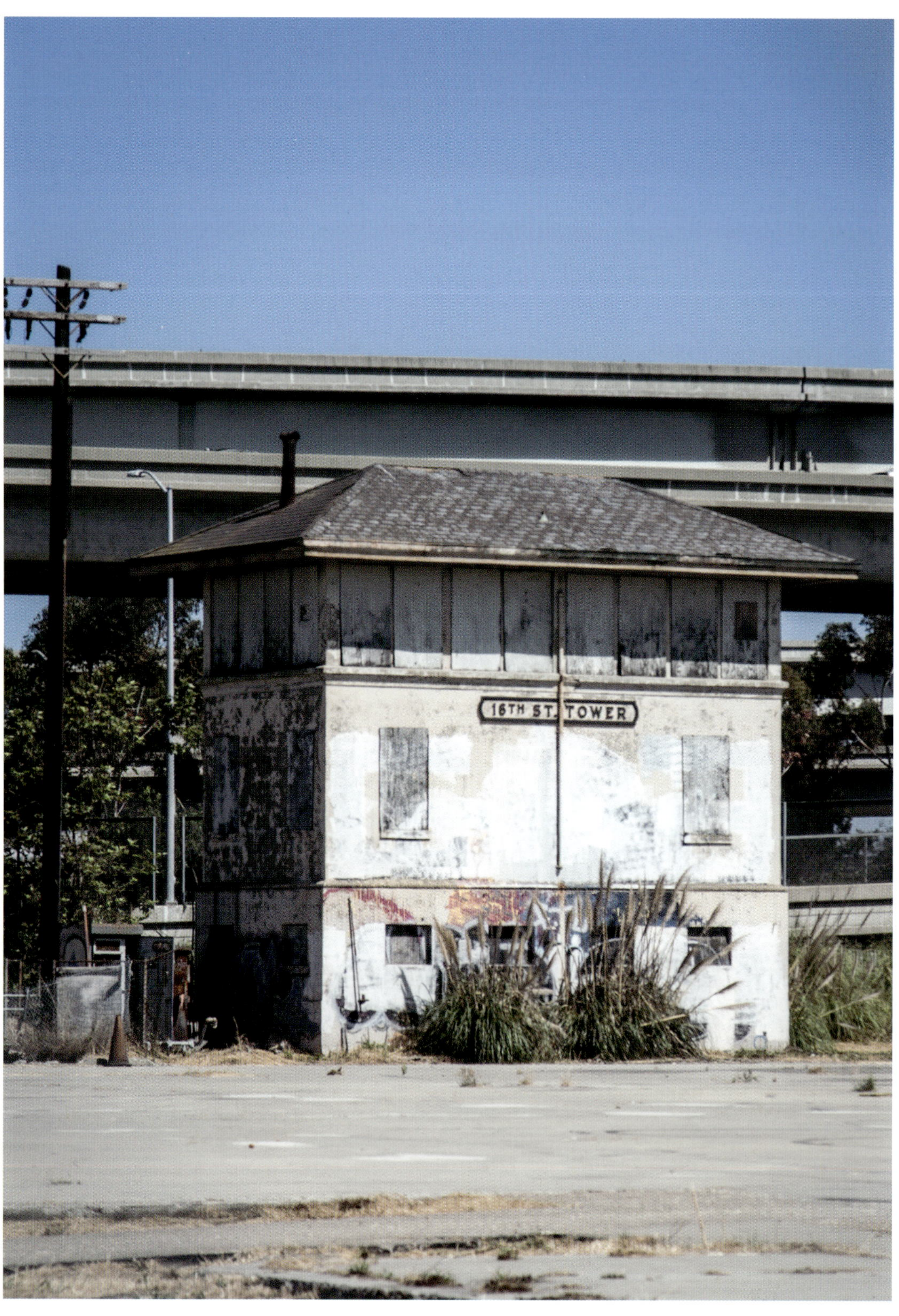

The abandoned 16th Street Tower.

3

THE ABANDONED SITES OF WINE COUNTRY

Though California's wine industry and vineyards usually conjure up images of glamour, stunning countryside landscapes, and indulgent afternoons of food and drink, there is another side to one of the state's most well-known regions and businesses. Whether it's an abandoned town in Sonoma, or the eerie, sprawling remains of one of the first major US wineries, some California history can also be gleaned from the land of grapes.

WINGO–SONOMA'S GHOST TOWN

Getting to Wingo is somewhat of a challenge; located deep in Sonoma County, Wingo is only accessible by a three-mile round-trip hike. Worse yet, the hike winds through windy, dusty trails leading from the nearest vineyard, through a marsh desert, to the abandoned town itself.

Wingo was built on the Sonoma Valley Creek as a stop for barges and steamboats to San Francisco; when I visited, the creek had completely dried up, courtesy of the repeated heat waves that had recently hit central and southern California.

The first structure you see as you approach the town is a rusty swing bridge, built originally for a monorail and eventually used by the local railroad. Further on, a few remaining houses, and a couple of structures that still look inhabited, form the tiny town. No more than ten or twelve total structures exist within the town limits.

Though no one knows exactly when this once popular town for ferry and railroad visitors was abandoned, the last record of a town resident was in 1994; a widow named Alice Mann was still living in the cabin she bought with her husband in 1956. Today, a couple of the buildings have cars and boats outside, but still look semi-abandoned. Located in the middle of endless fields of family-owned vineyards, Wingo looks disturbingly out of place, but fascinating nonetheless.

WINEHAVEN

The impressive sprawling complex of Winehaven, set on 412 acres in Richmond, California, is a former winery that once housed almost 400 workers at its peak. The California Wine Association purchased the property and built the enormous winery after the 1906 San Francisco earthquake, which all but destroyed the association's previous South of Market headquarters.

The seven San Francisco wine merchants that formed the association at that time, who held 85% of the state's wine market, had built an international reputation for the California wine industry, which had been virtually unknown outside the state just a decade prior. Winehaven quickly flourished, becoming known as the world's largest winery for twelve years, from 1907 to 1919. It shipped almost 500,000 gallons of its wine products a month all over the world.

Unfortunately, in 1919, the passage of Prohibition shut the winery down, and it remained abandoned for a couple of decades with the exception of a small post office that operated on its grounds.

Eventually, the Navy bought the property in 1941 and used it as a fuel depot, though it left the original buildings of the winery largely untouched. Many of them are now in the National Register, including the impressive Winehaven Building with its towering turrets.

The abandoned buildings are on private property, so their interiors are not easily accessible, but travelers can still marvel at the immense size of Winehaven, the architecture of the central building, and the sheer number of remaining homes that used to house the winery's workers.

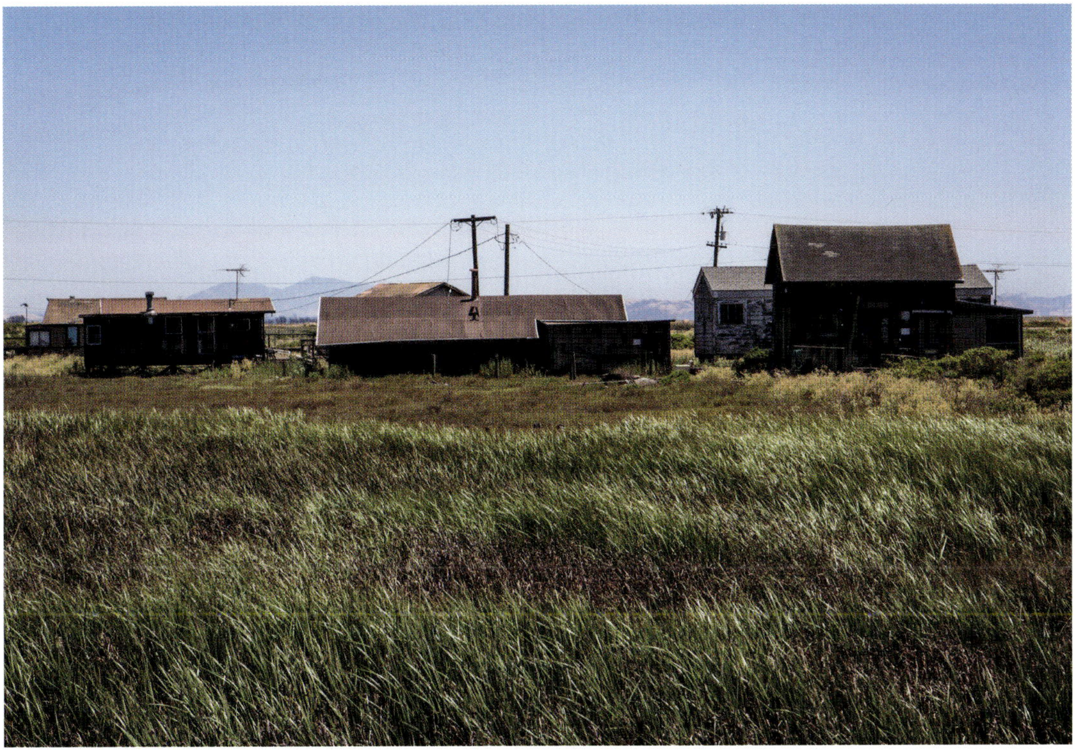

The first sight of Wingo from a distance.

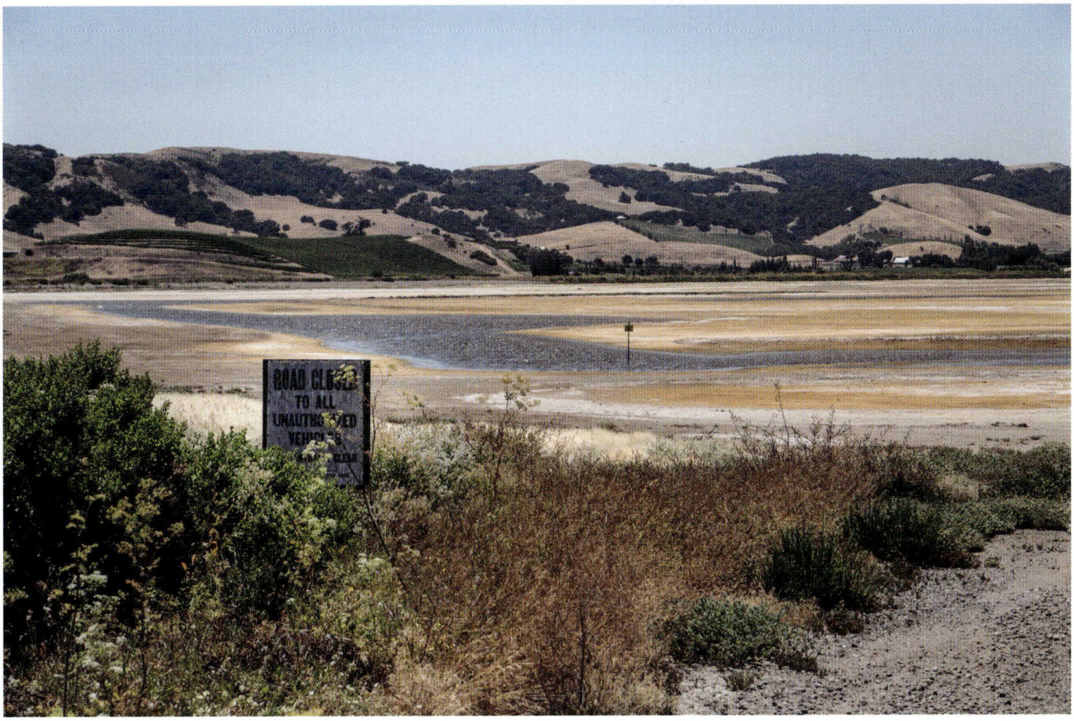

The roads to Wingo have been closed down, so no car traffic can pass through.

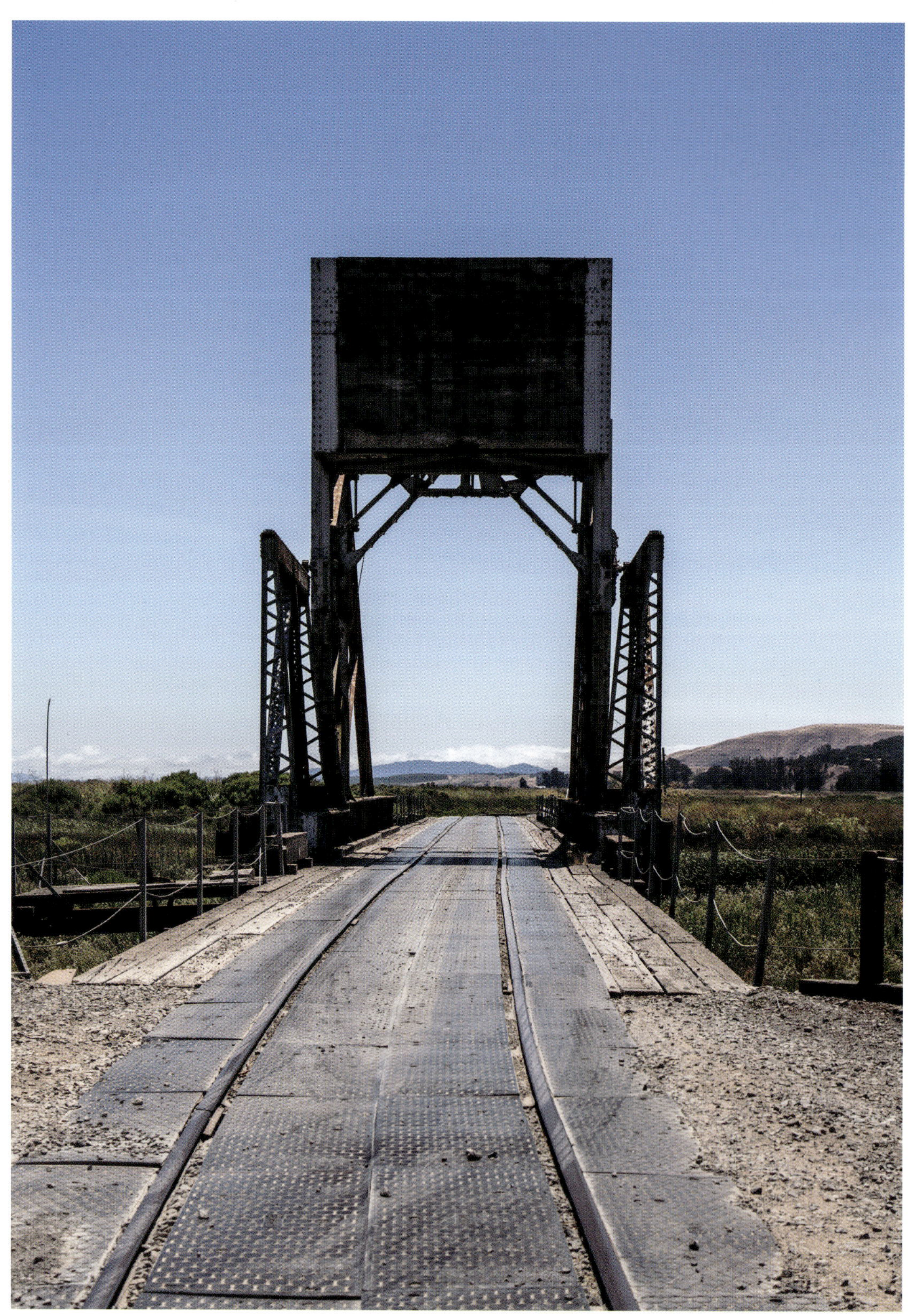

The swing bridge at the entrance of Wingo.

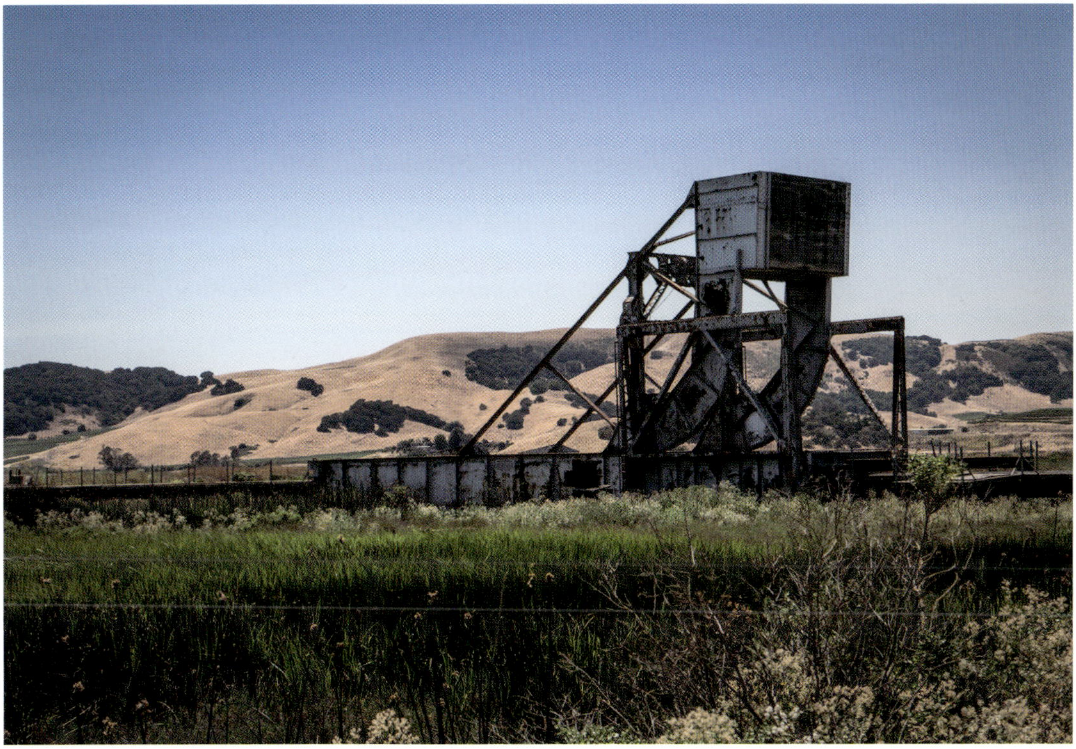

A distant view of the town's swing bridge.

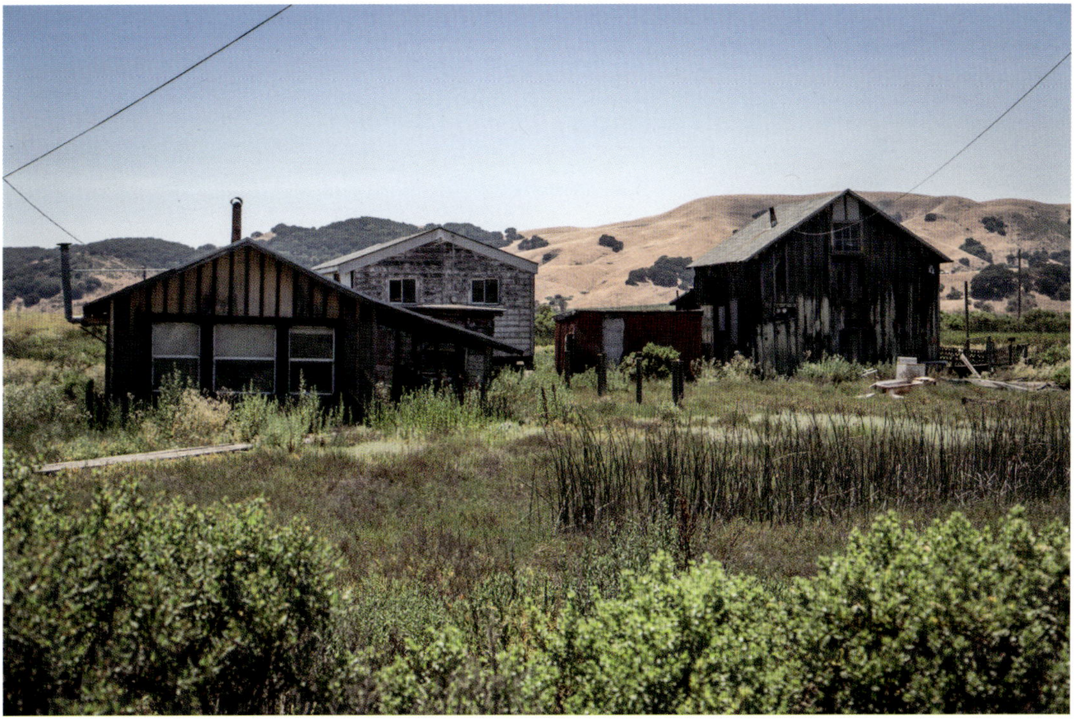

Getting closer to the few remaining houses in Wingo.

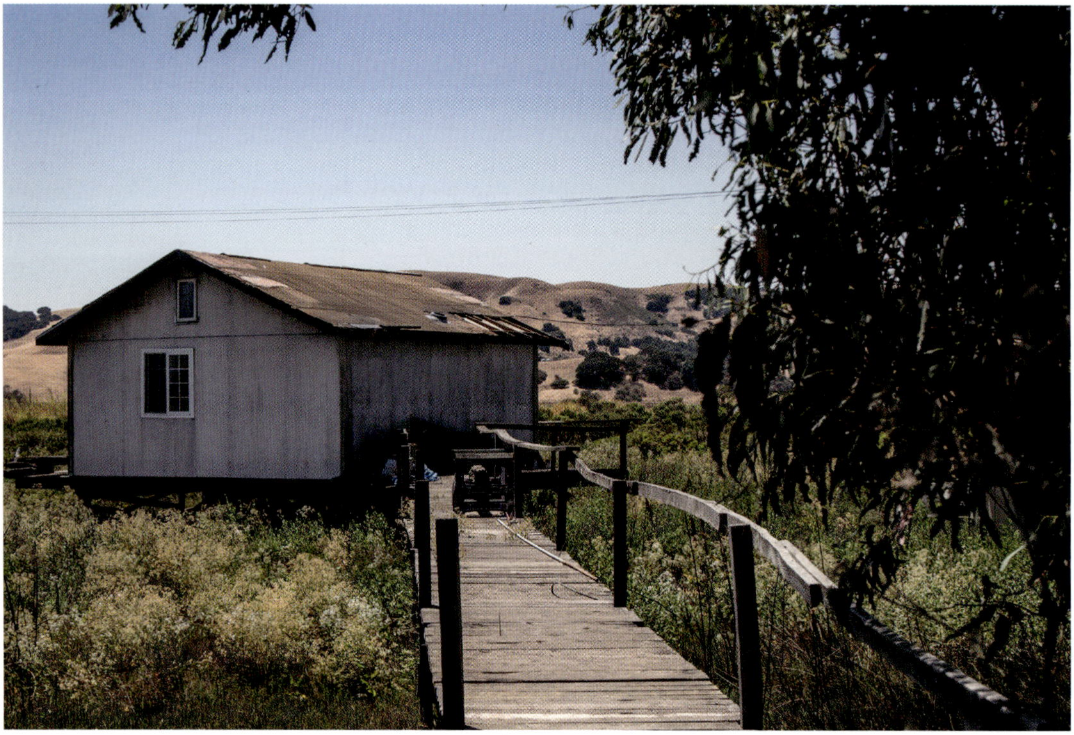

This walkway was probably built to cross over the creek that has now dried up.

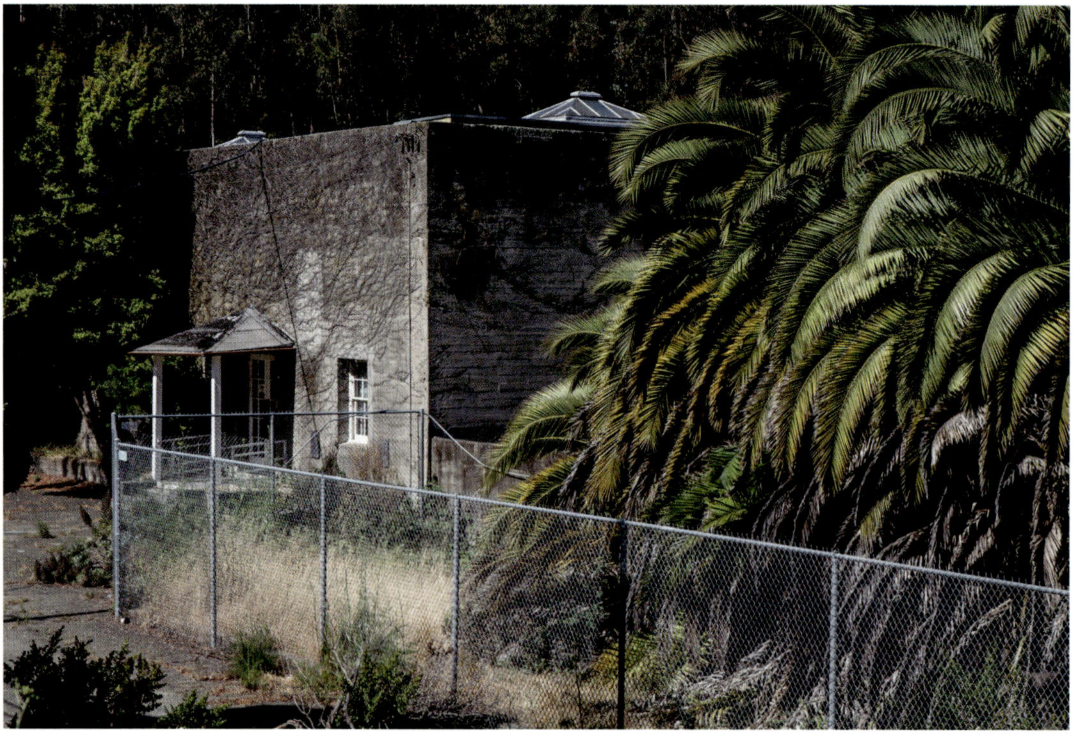

One of the main Winehaven buildings; all are inaccessible to visitors.

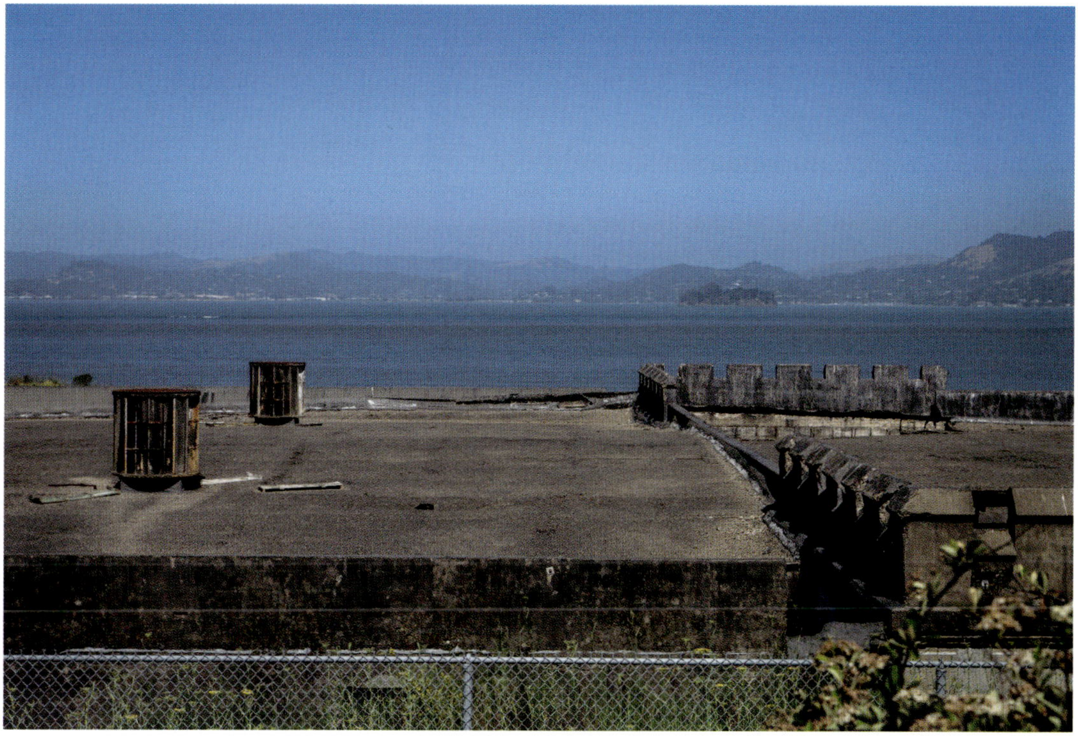

The top of the Winehaven winery, with turrets jutting out and a sea view.

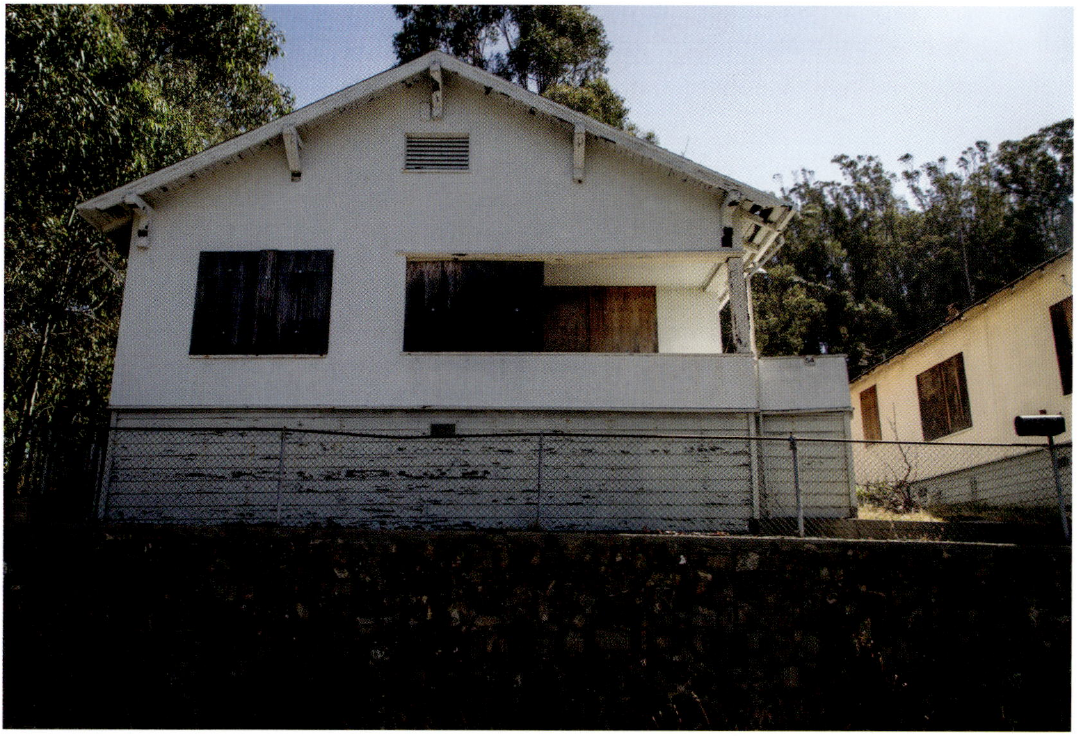

A former winery worker's house.

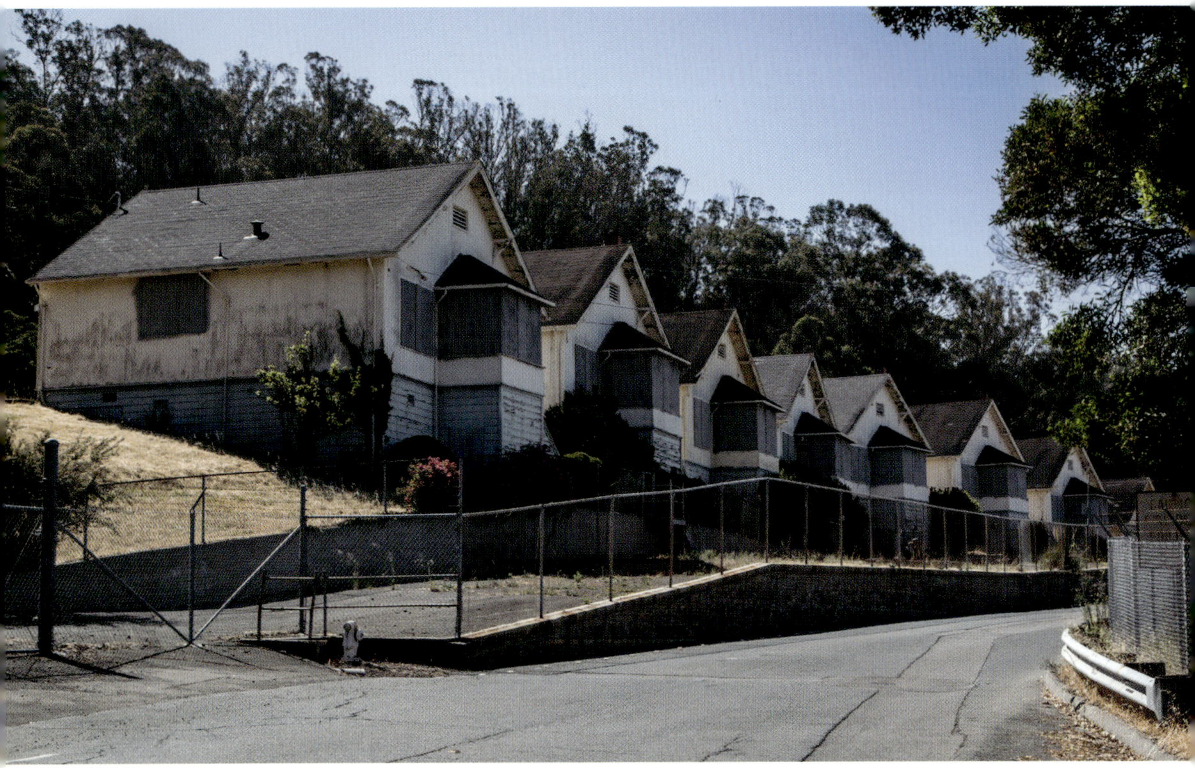

A row of housing for winery workers at Winehaven.

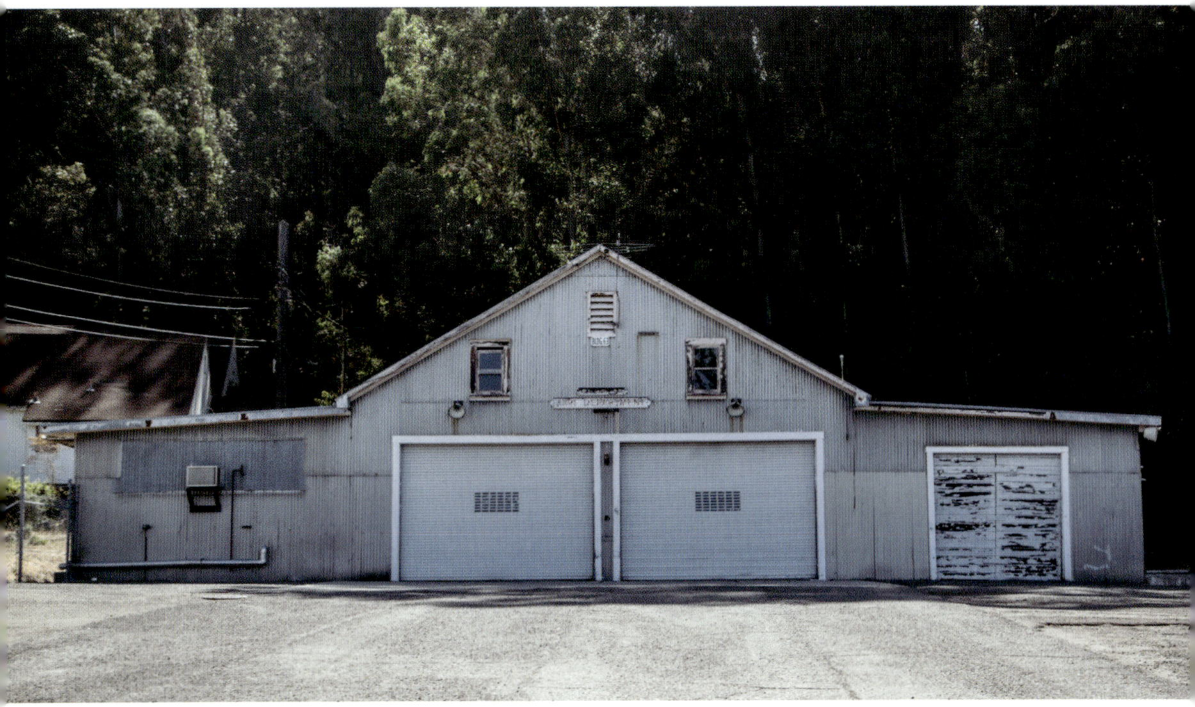

An abandoned fire station for the Winehaven community.

4

INNOVATION AND INSPIRATION IN THE WEST

From Hollywood to Silicon Valley, California has always served as an inspiration to many creative individuals, inventors, and entrepreneurs from all over the world. This was just as true 100 years ago as it is today, as the stories of mold-breaking individuals like author Jack London and inventor Guglielmo Marconi show.

No one knows exactly why California serves as such an inspiration to so many; perhaps the state's majestic nature encourages creativity and art, or the pioneering mindset of those who immigrate here drive innovation and progress. Traveling through the central California forests and then down the Pacific Coast, you will come across little-known artifacts and abandoned remains from the lives of innovative individuals whose words and works influenced the United States (and the world) for years after their deaths.

JACK LONDON'S WOLF HOUSE—A WILDERNESS RETREAT

Nestled in the forest of Jack London Historic State Park, Wolf House, the famous nature-loving author's dream house, remains as a skeletal, abandoned structure deep in the California woods. The name of the dwelling arises from the nickname for London himself —"The Wolf."

London wrote so many books about wolves and wilderness that the nickname for himself and his house seemed appropriate; after all, two of his most well-known titles are *White Fang* and *The Call of the Wild*. It was clear in his interviews and writing that nature and beauty was of paramount importance to him, hence the private, undisturbed location of his ideal home in the middle of a pristine forest.

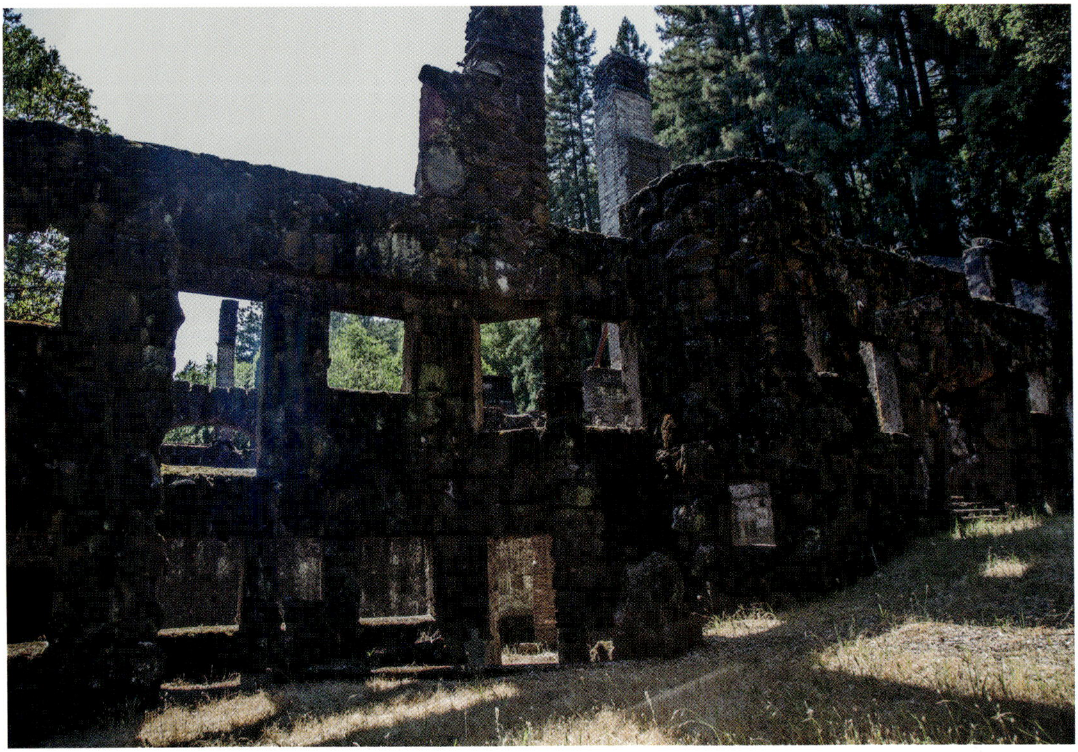

Light shines through the empty window openings of Wolf House.

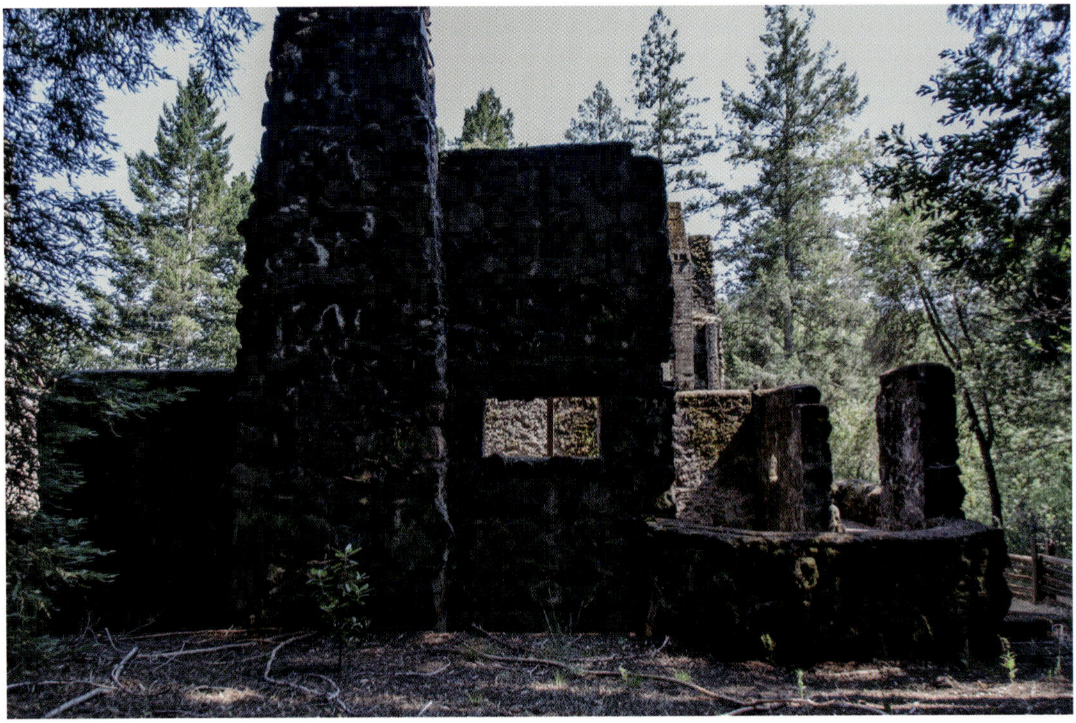

One of the preserved Wolf House structures.

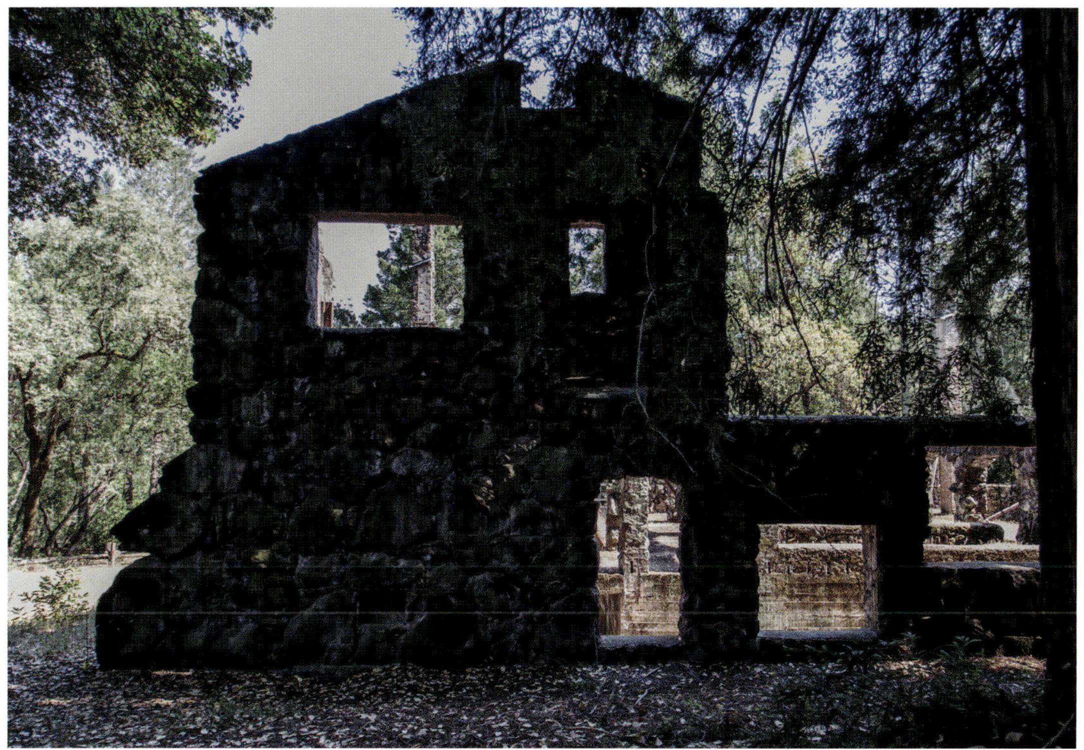

One of the stone walls of Wolf House.

> I write for no other purpose than to add to the beauty that now belongs to me. I write a book for no other reason than to add three or four hundred acres to my magnificent estate.
>
> Jack London

Sadly enough, London never got to actually live in his ideal home. After he started building Wolf House in 1911, and construction was almost completed by the summer of 1913, a fire started and spread throughout the house, burning down most of the completed interior.

London swore he would rebuild the house, and had he lived longer, he may have. Sadly, the prolific author died shortly after in the area (Glen Ellen) in 1916. His gravesite is a short hike from Wolf House; he requested his ashes be placed near the grave of two pioneer children, and his wife's ashes were placed there as well when she died after him.

Nevertheless, the location and structure of the house give an idea of what a beautiful dwelling it may have been had things gone differently. As part of the abandoned exhibit, you can even see the original floor plan that shows what might have been, how the layout and interior would have looked had London lived to see the structure completed and inhabited.

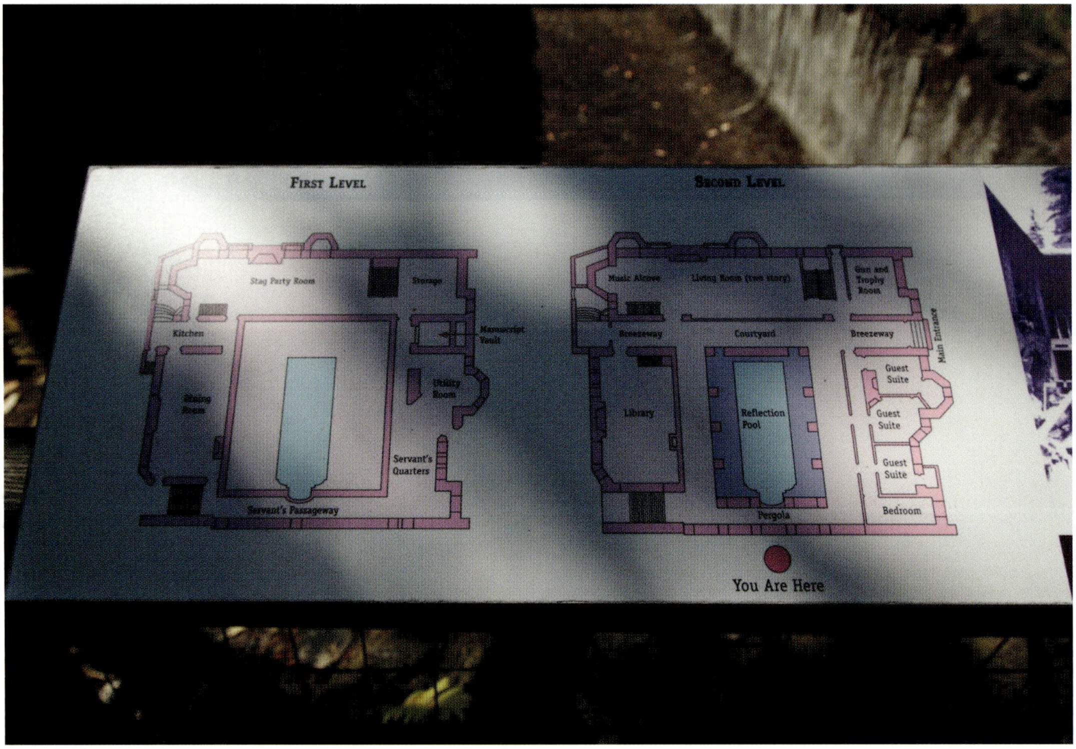

The original design for the house shows what might have been.

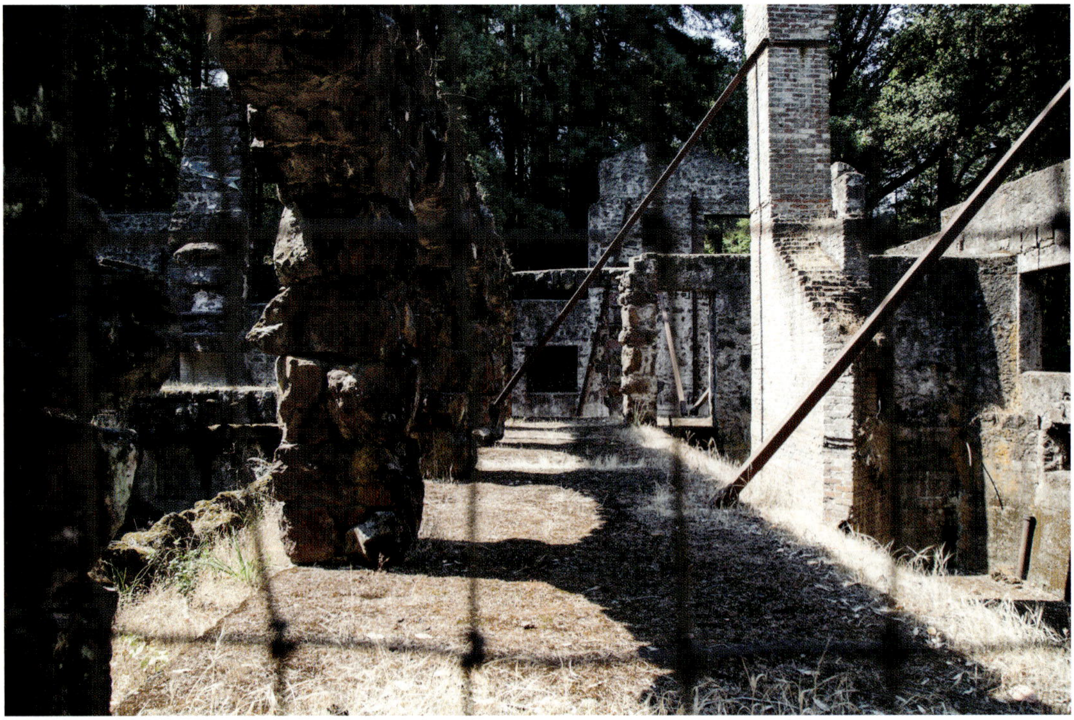

Looking into what would have been a hallway.

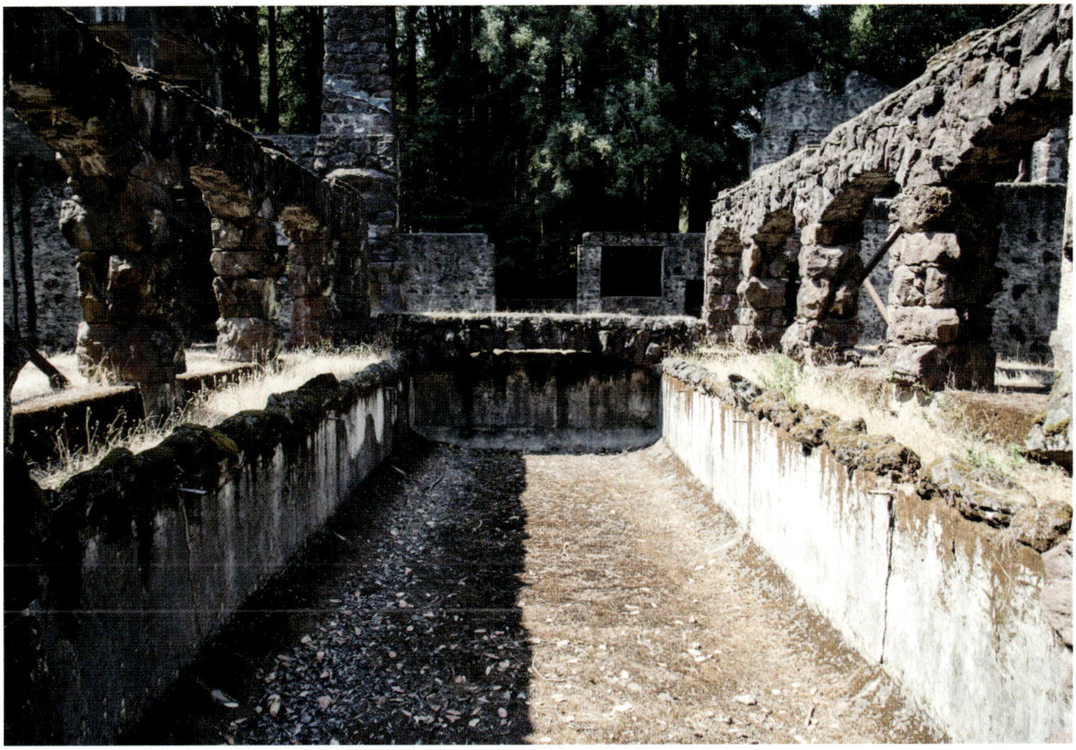

The house's original courtyard/pool area.

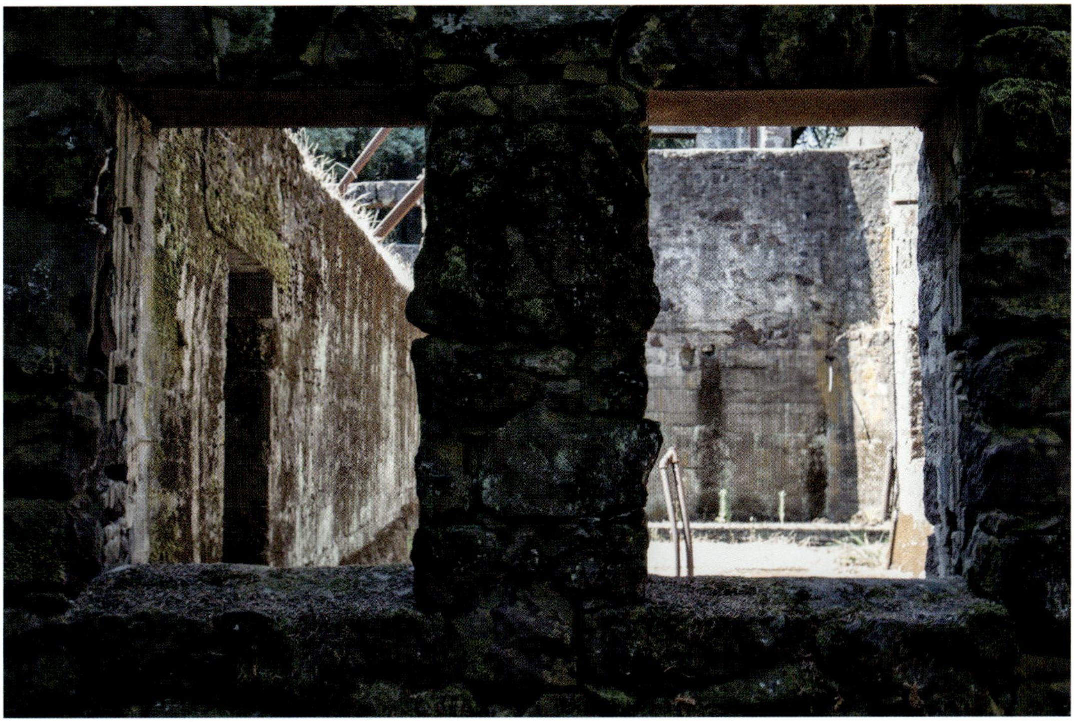

Looking through window openings to the rest of the house's skeleton.

MARCONI HOTEL

The Marconi Hotel has an intriguing history and even stranger current existence. This abandoned, elegant, ivy-covered structure on the Pacific coast sits next to a functioning, modern convention center, seeming very odd and out of place in this context.

Named after the inventor of radio, Guglielmo Marconi, the structure was originally built in 1913-1914 as a hotel for Marconi's staff at his radio receiving station. At the time, the hotel was the epitome of luxury, containing a library, game room, lounge, and dining hall. Some of its past opulence is still visible in its design and interiors.

Soon after its construction, the military moved in during World War I to take over Marconi's transmitters for the war effort. This move, and therefore this hotel, actually played a pivotal role in scientific history, as it led to Marconi losing his tight grip on worldwide radio transmissions.

The fate of the hotel would then take a strange turn in the 1960s after being taken over by Synanon, which was ostensibly a rehab facility but actually turned out to be a cult, or "alternative lifestyle community." The facility baptized itself the "Church of Synanon" in 1975. Rumors of strange laws and orders within the cult started to circulate, including forced vasectomies for men, which eventually turned out to be mostly true. After their leader was charged with attempted murder, and the church was accused of hoarding weapons, the entire operation was shut down in 1980 and the building was left abandoned.

Despite its bizarre history, it is impossible not to admire the classic beauty of the Marconi Hotel, still visible through the thick vegetation that has grown over it and the many years that have worn away at its walls.

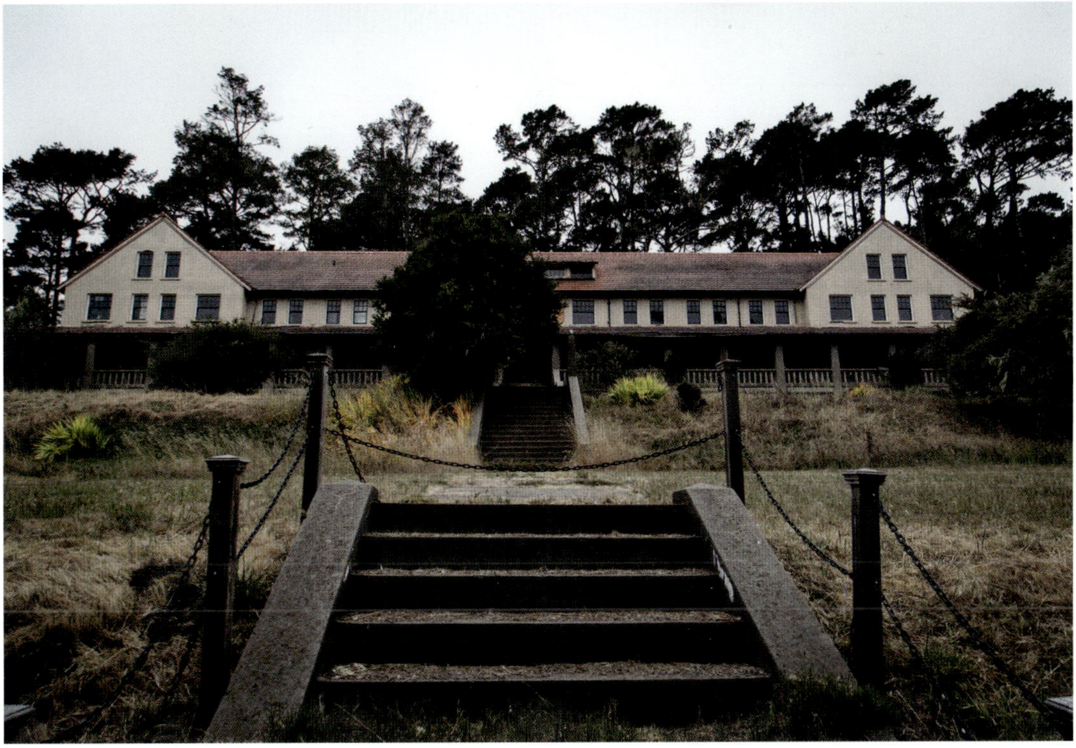

Walking up to the Marconi Hotel.

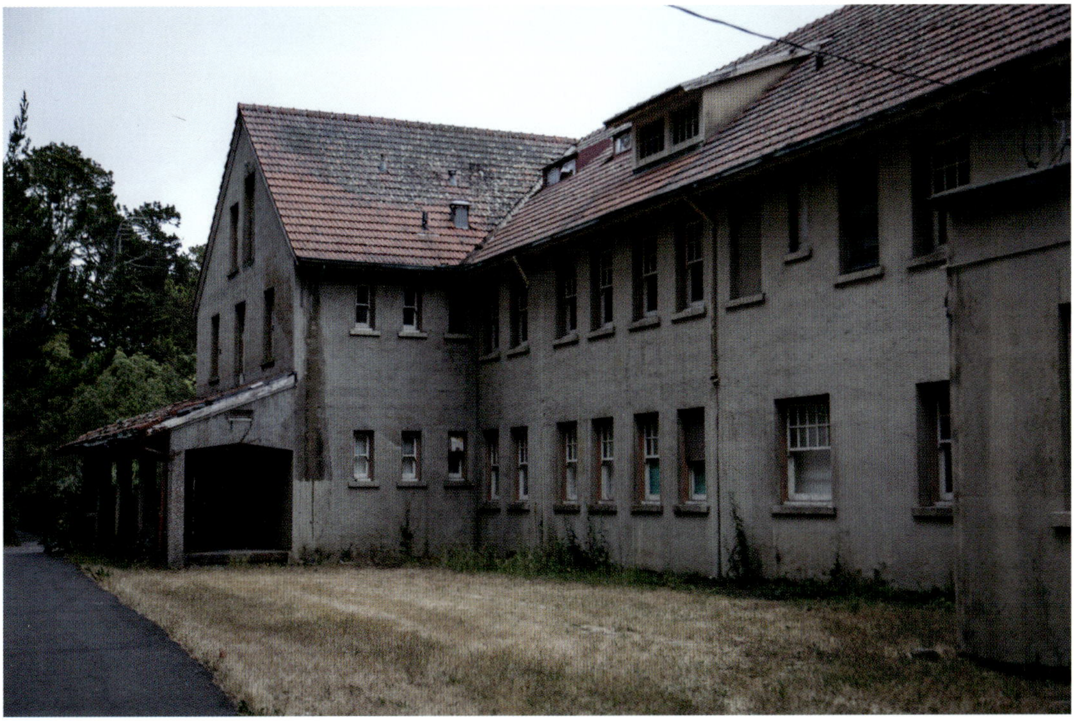

The ivy-covered back entrance to the Marconi Hotel.

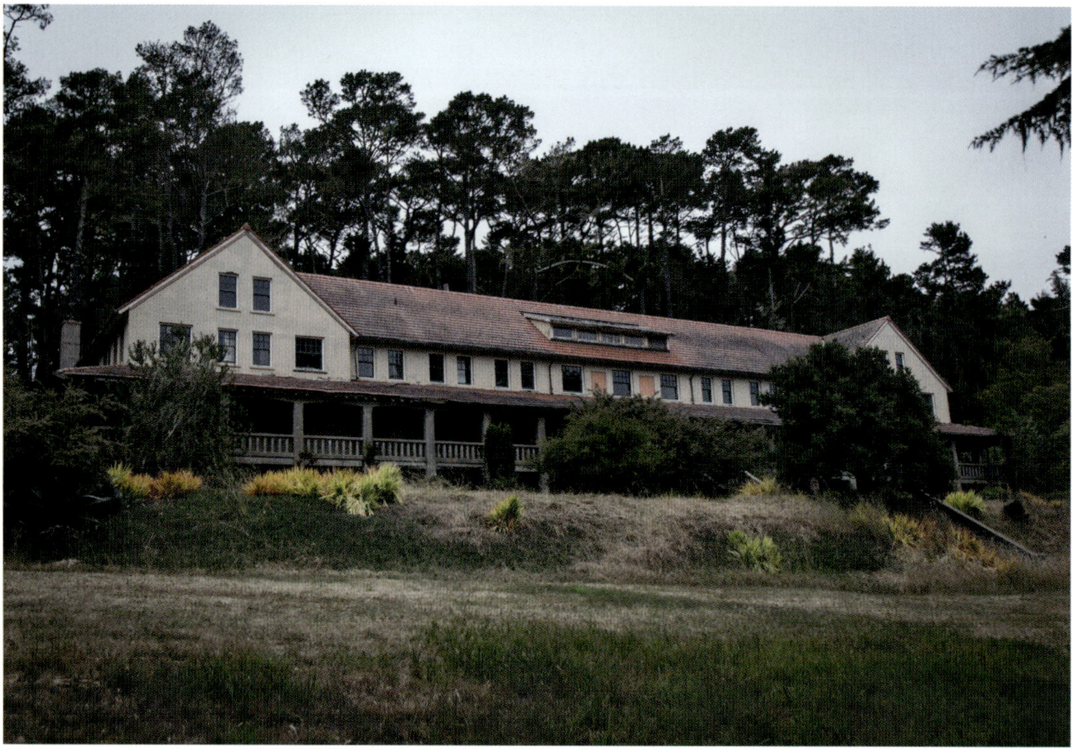

First view of the Marconi Hotel's exterior.

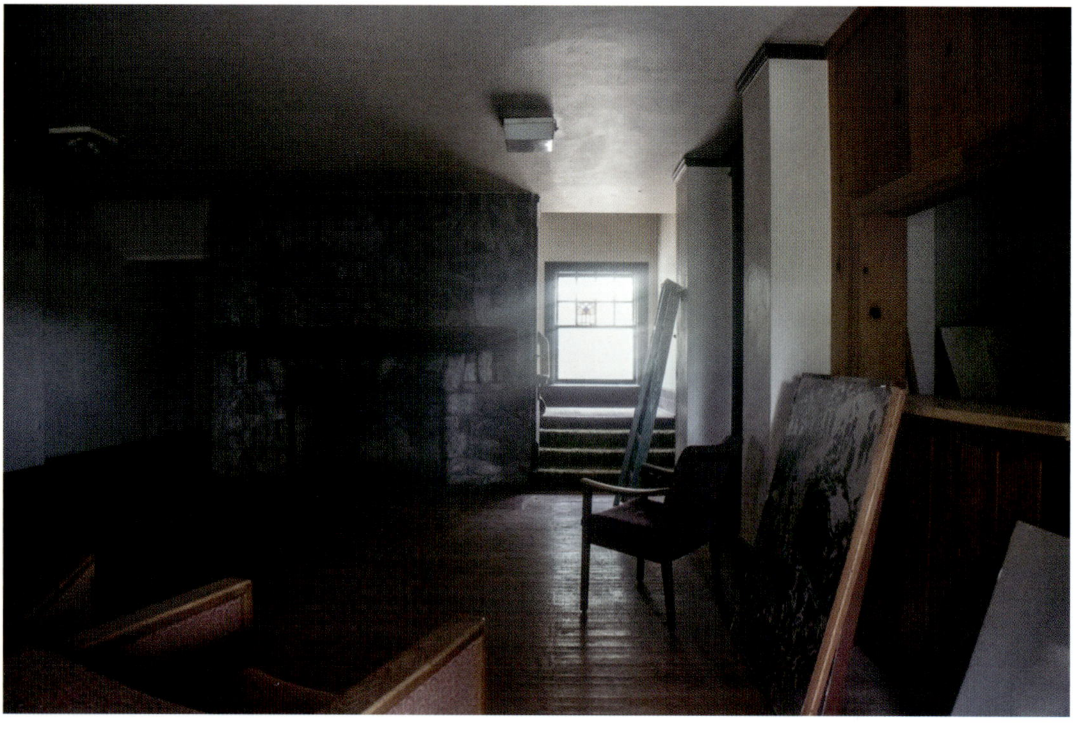

Looking into the entrance hall/former lobby of the former hotel.

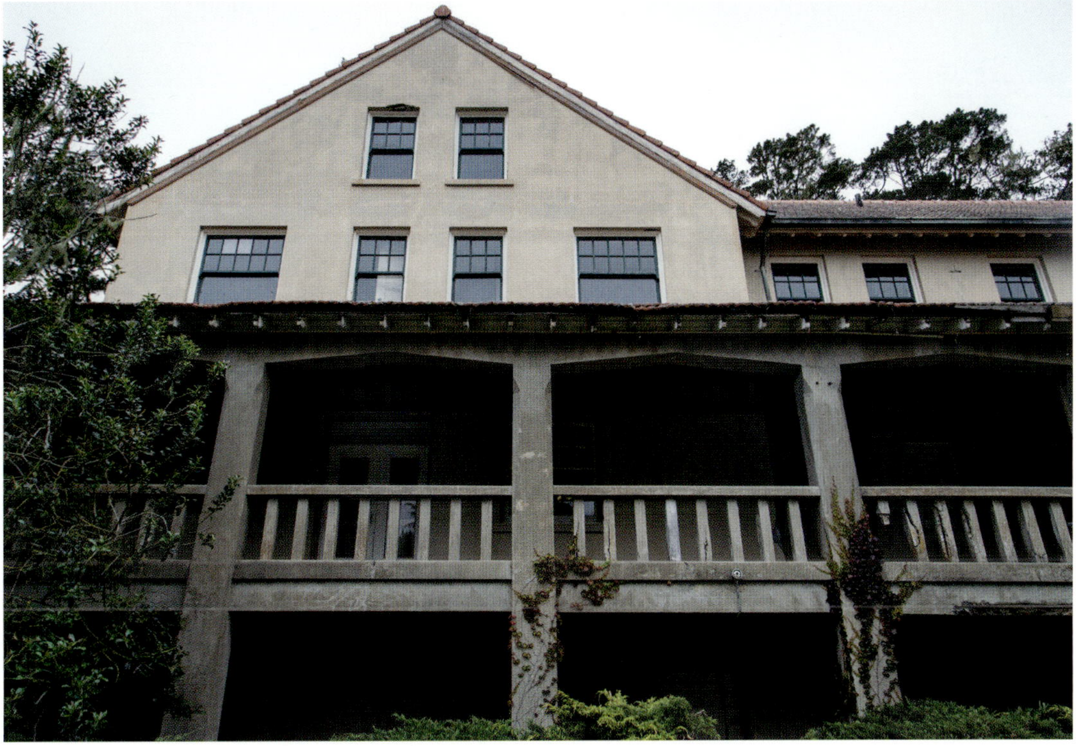

Looking at the building's formerly elegant exteriors.

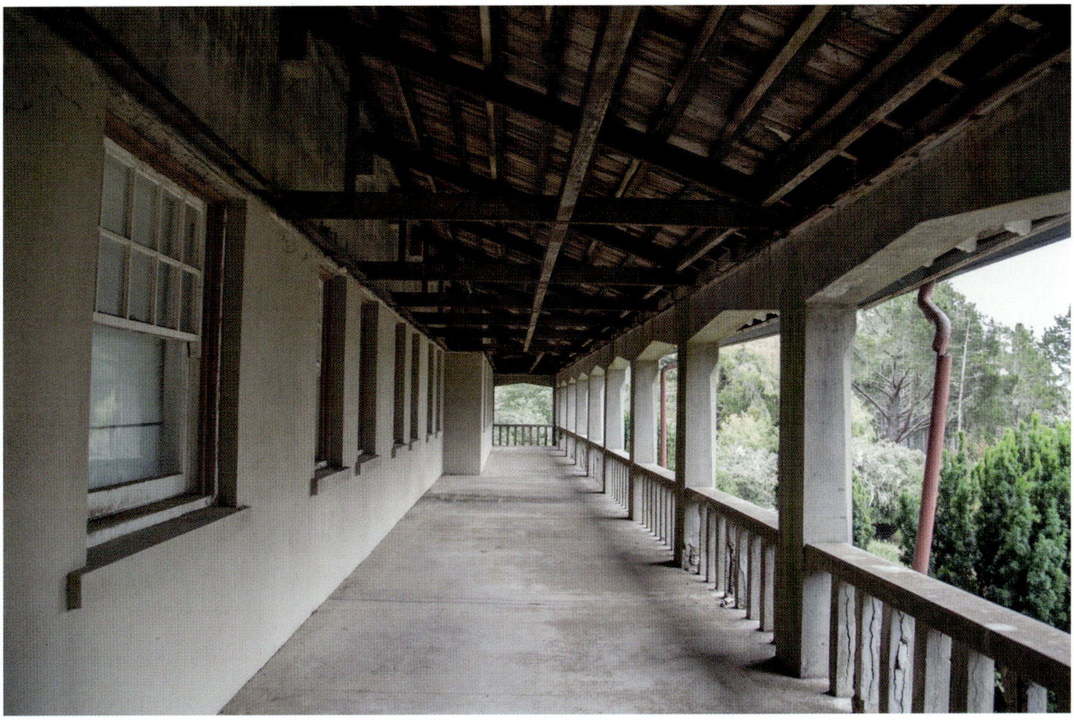

The outside patio of the Marconi Hotel.

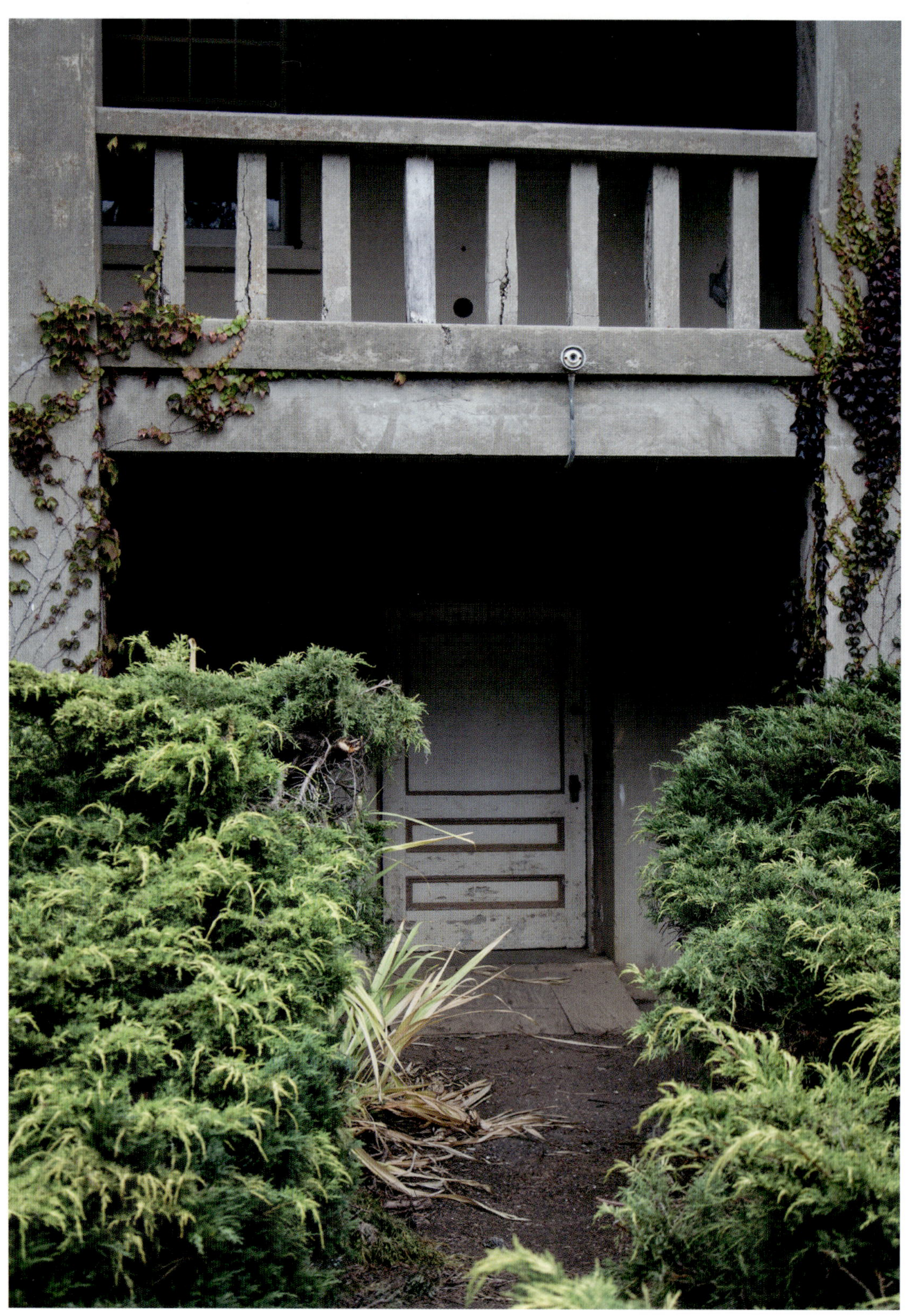

All entrances to the Marconi Hotel are bolted shut.

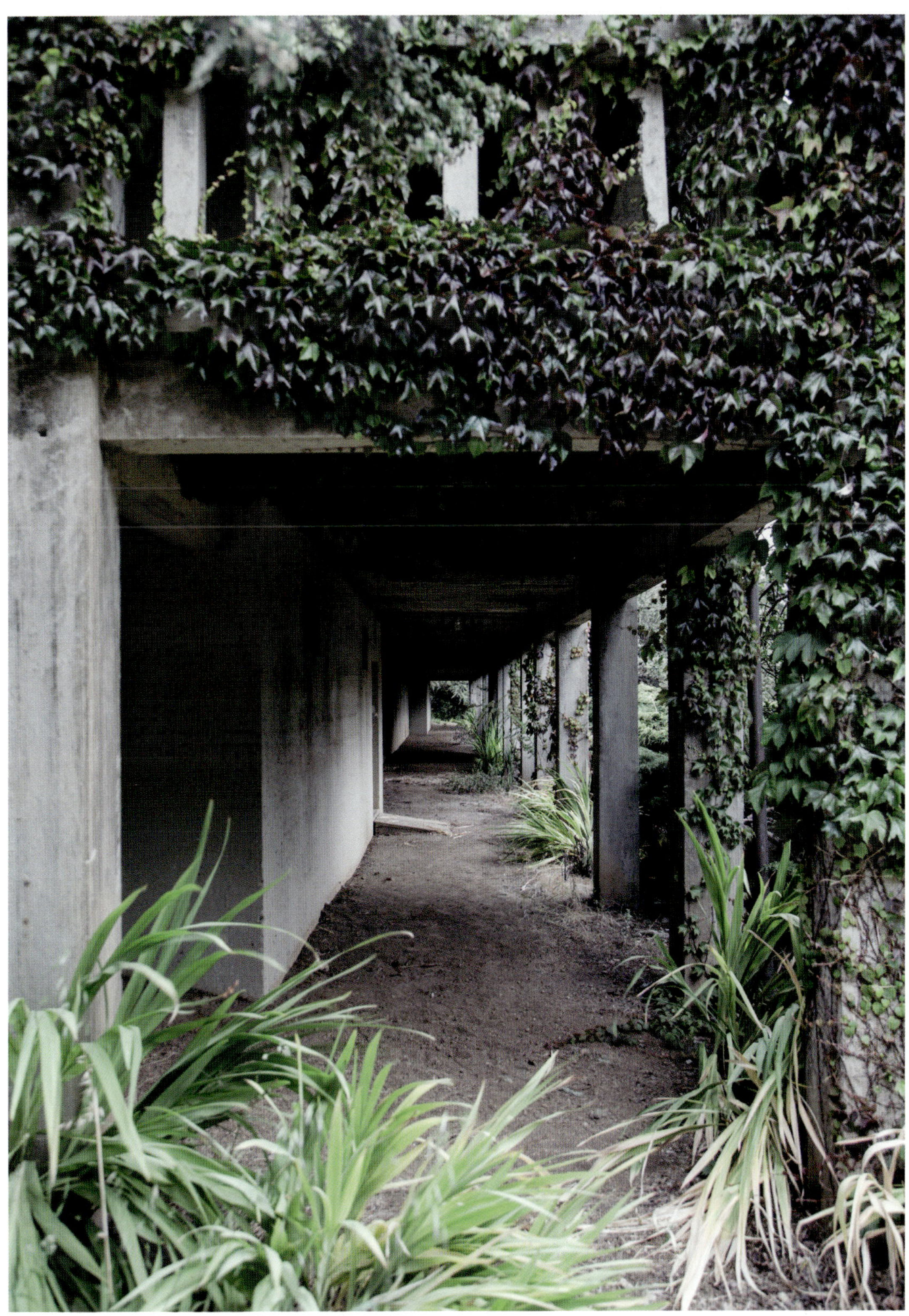

Vines and ivy cover most of the structure.

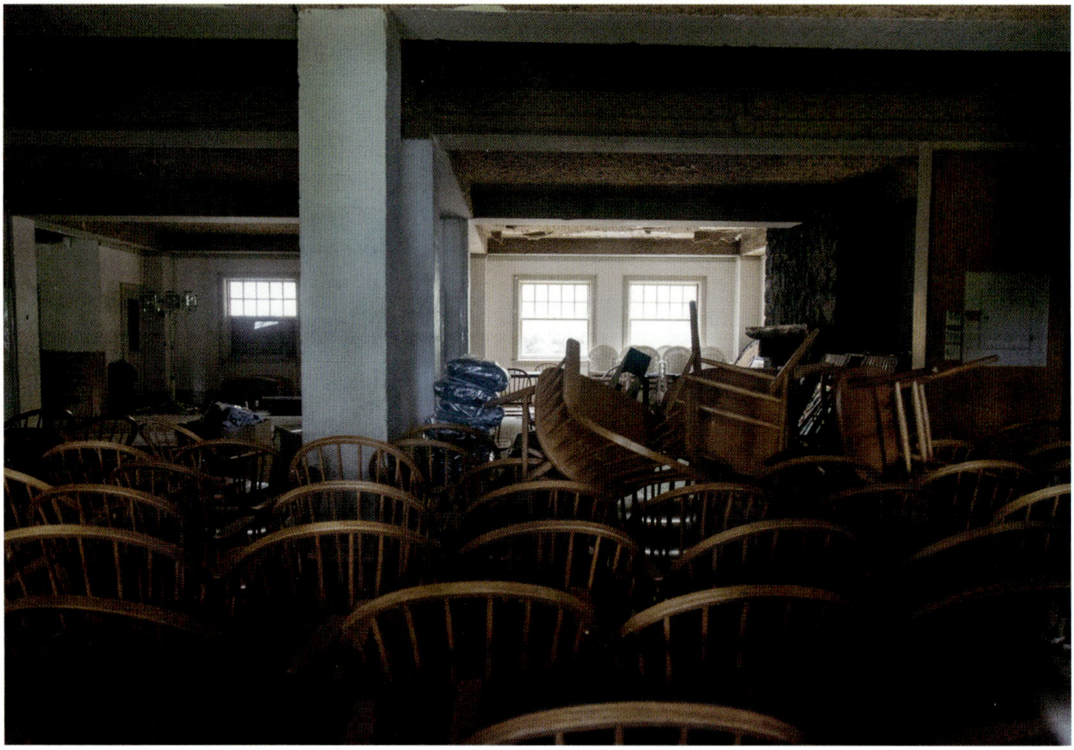

Chairs remain stacked up in a former meeting space.

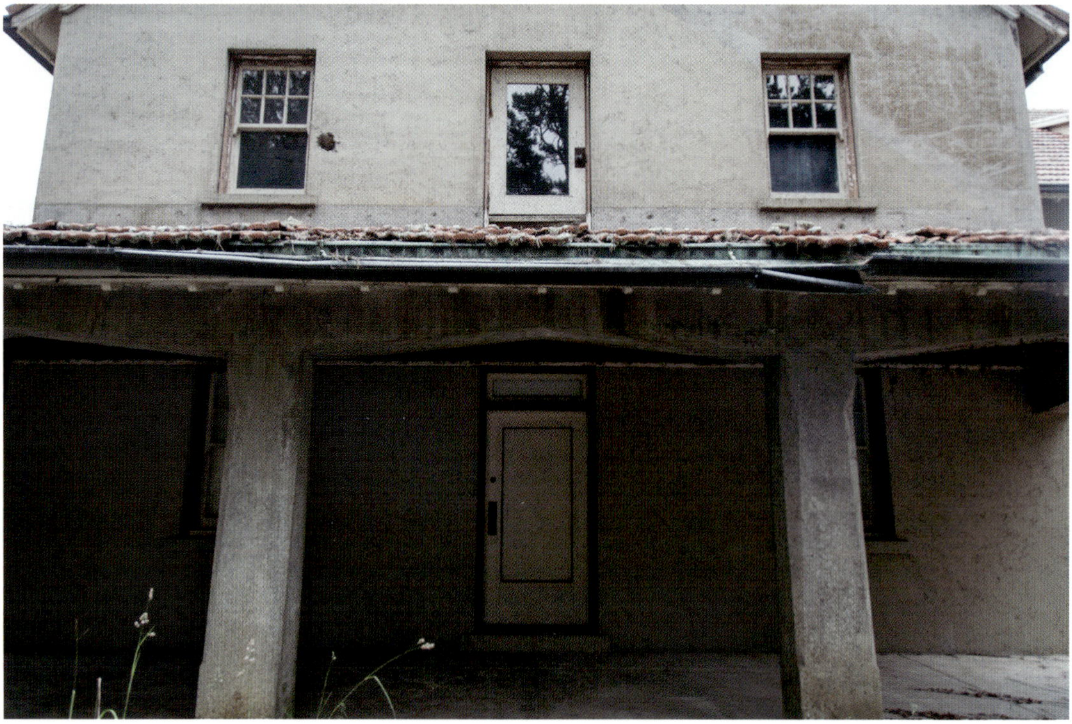

The kitchen entrance to the hotel.

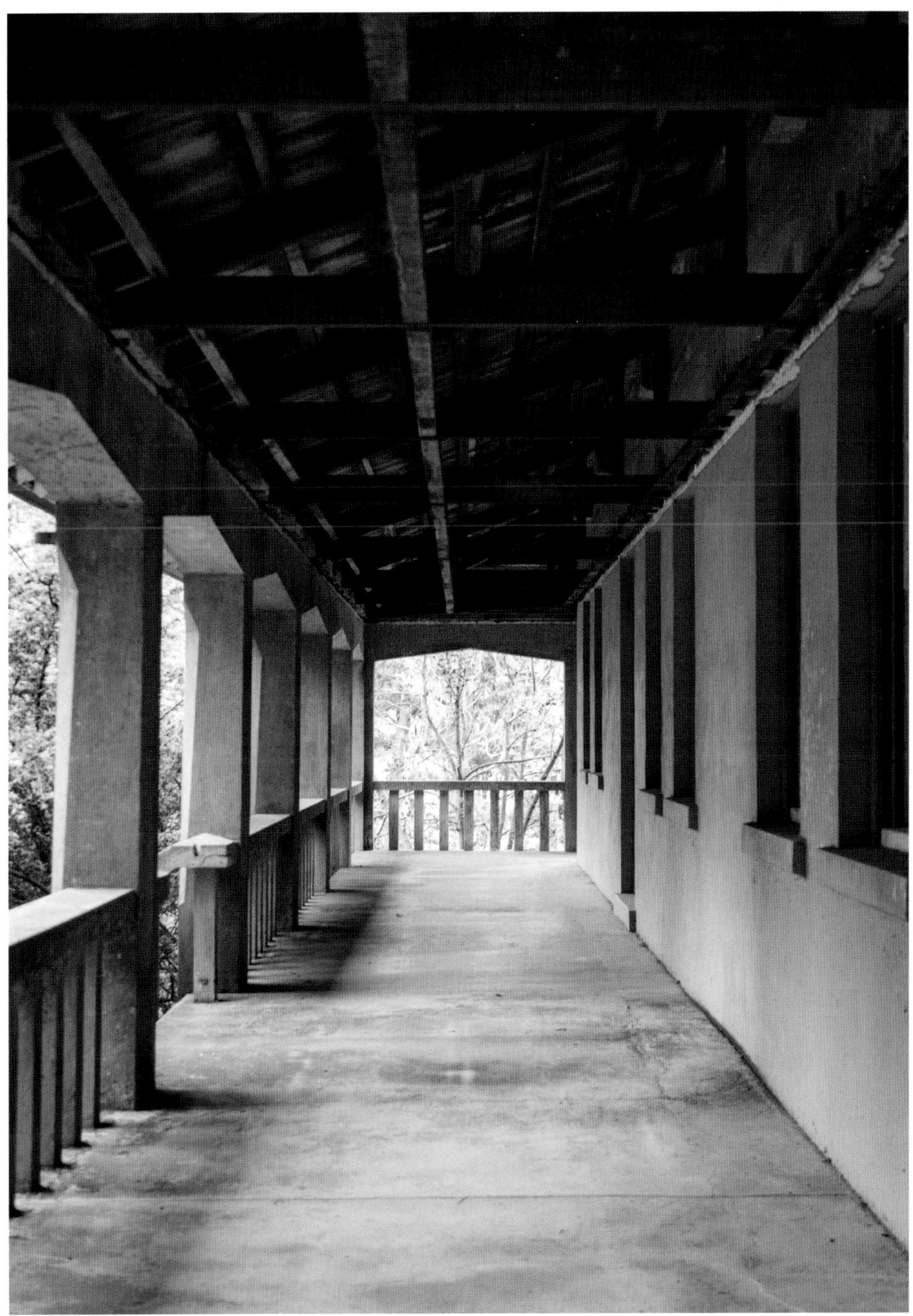

Patios wrap around the beautifully designed, now abandoned hotel.

5

MILITARY BUILDUP ON THE WEST COAST

Due to its location on the West Coast, magnificent natural harbor, and importance as an urban center, San Francisco historically had many military and naval centers built in its periphery in order to protect the city and serve as bases for potential military attacks.

The city served as a main port and shipyard for the US Navy, in part due to the fact that for most of California history, San Francisco was much larger than other West Coast metropolises, including Los Angeles, Seattle, and San Diego. After the attack on Pearl Harbor, renewed focus on military bases and protection for the West Coast increased San Francisco's military prominence even further.

However, with the advent of better long-range military technology and the drop in threats to the West Coast, San Francisco became less crucial to the US defense strategy over time. These developments allowed bases to be moved into the desert or down into harbors such as San Diego, where the navy didn't have to share space with commercial shipping. This is why many bases and military complexes in San Francisco and the Bay Area lie abandoned.

ALAMEDA NAVAL BASE

Originally built as an airport for the city of Alameda, the Alameda Naval Base was created after the land was given to the US government in 1936. After purchasing the property, the government constructed facilities for naval aviation, initially just enough for two carrier air wings, five seaplane squadrons, and two utility squadrons.

The start of World War II led to changes in Alameda, and eventually the base became the headquarters for a complex system of auxiliary airfields. Alameda provided aviation support for San Francisco, which was the major Western naval surface and supply base at the time.

The Pearl Harbor attack and subsequent US involvement against Japan increased the significance of the Alameda base, as it then became a center for handling logistics regarding moving planes, personnel, and equipment from Europe to the Pacific in order to engage Japan.

Alameda Naval Base continued to operate during the Cold War, due to the need to protect the West Coast, but was eventually closed in 1997.

NAVAL STATION TREASURE ISLAND

In the little visited corner of the Bay Area known as Treasure Island sits an abandoned naval station, known (appropriately enough) as Naval Station Treasure Island.

Though many people in the area spend their lives without ever once turning off onto the Treasure Island exit from the nearby bridge as they commute between San Francisco and Oakland, the area is actually home to some intriguing local military history.

Neighboring Yerba Buena Island is a naturally occurring island, but Treasure Island is man-made, built from sediments in the bay in 1936 in order to host the Golden Gate International Exposition Worlds Fair. In 1941, the Navy acquired the property and built up a huge facility, motivated in part by the start of World War II and the need to build up the country's military. At its peak, Naval Station Treasure Island was processing around 12,000 military personnel a day either going overseas for military service or returning from abroad. After World War II, the station still operated at a high capacity, with 3,000 military and 1,000 civilian personnel working in the facility.

The Naval Station was shut down in 1997 and put aside for redevelopment. However, after a massive oil spill in 2007 from the container ship *Cosco Busan*, the Navy is still completing environmental cleanup actions in the area, which has delayed the conversion of the base to any other purpose. Many toxic chemicals escaped into the waters right off the Treasure Island coast, creating major health and environmental concerns.

Authorities also have concerns now about the stability of the island. When it was initially built, Treasure Island was 14 feet above sea level, but has now sunk to approximately 9 feet above sea level. Any major earthquake or landslide could result in widespread damage to the buildings, or irreversible destruction to the island's foundation.

If you visit Treasure Island nowadays, you will come upon the abandoned naval buildings, in addition to a few (very few) office buildings that appear to currently be in use. School signs and crossings are obvious throughout the grounds, as well as buildings designated for educational purposes. Though some of these might have been for the military personnel's families, an enormous Fleet Training Center was also included in the Naval Station when it was operational.

BATTERY SPENCER

Perched high up on the Marin Headlands, looking out at San Francisco across the bay, is Battery Spencer. The concrete structure was built in 1893, with construction completed in 1897, as one of many protection points for San Francisco created to protect the harbor militarily.

Named after Revolutionary War hero Major General Joseph Spencer, Battery Spencer was armed with multiple 12-inch rifles and guns that the military could use to defend the harbor, until the weapons were scrapped during World War II for the war effort. Multiple rooms throughout the battery, that can still be seen today, were used to house either shells and ammunition or generators to keep the base going.

The abandoned military structure still remains, and is now one of the best places in the Bay Area from which to view the iconic Golden Gate Bridge with San Francisco in the background.

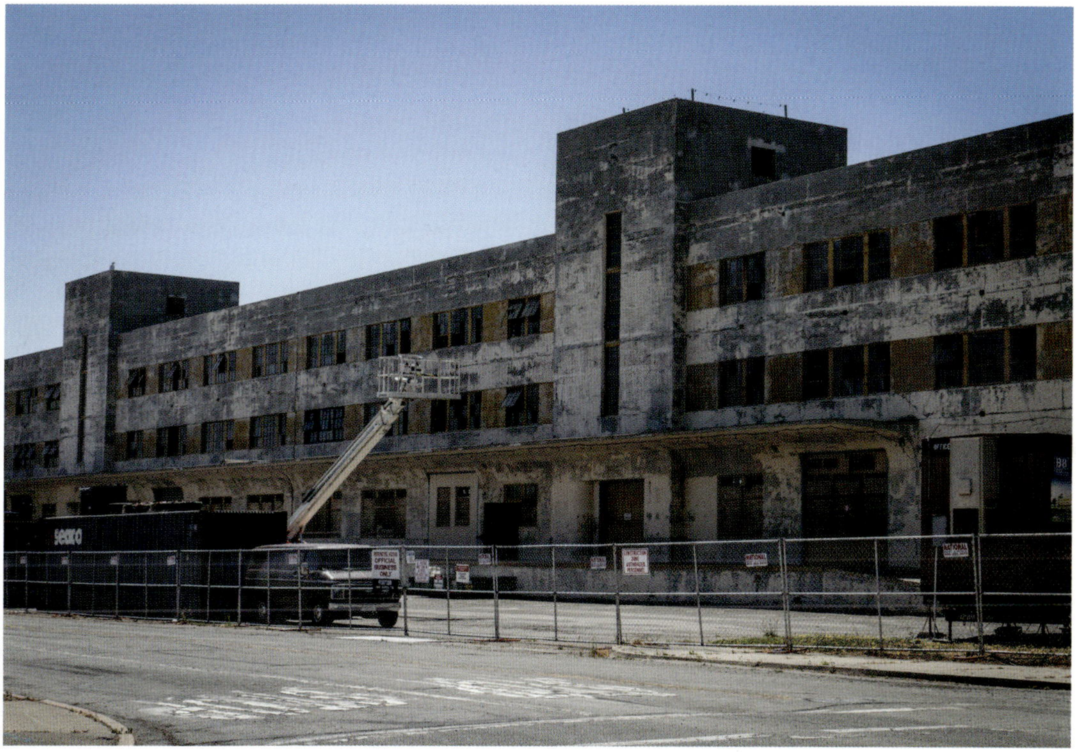

Some structures at Alameda Naval Base have decayed much faster than others.

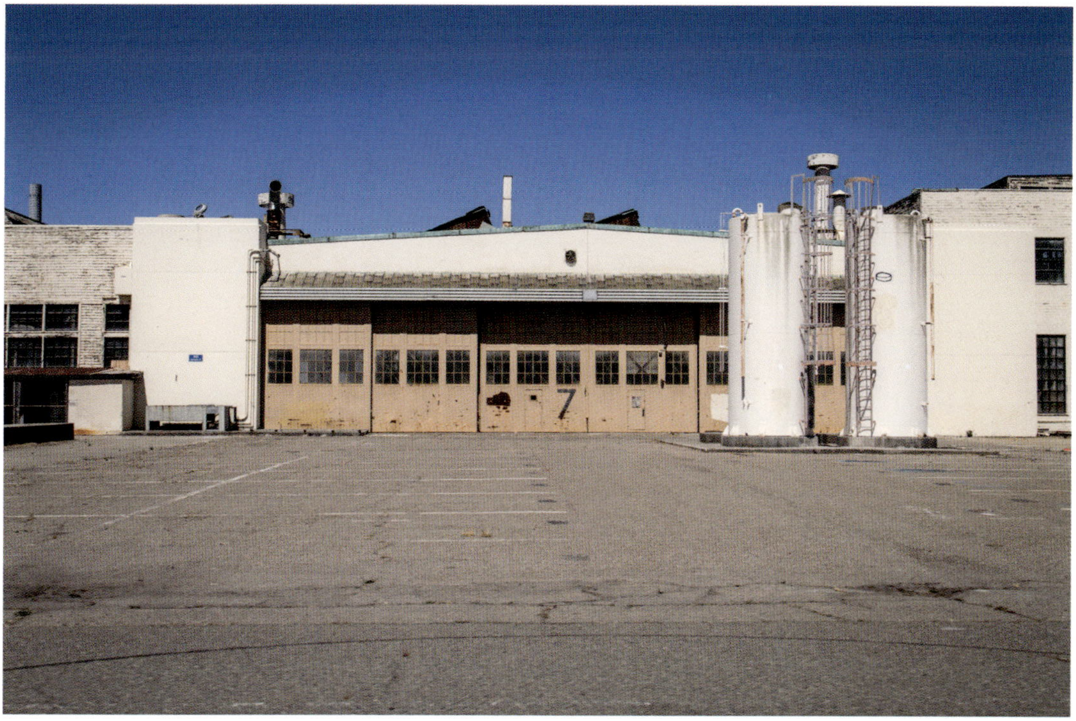

A former storage facility for military equipment.

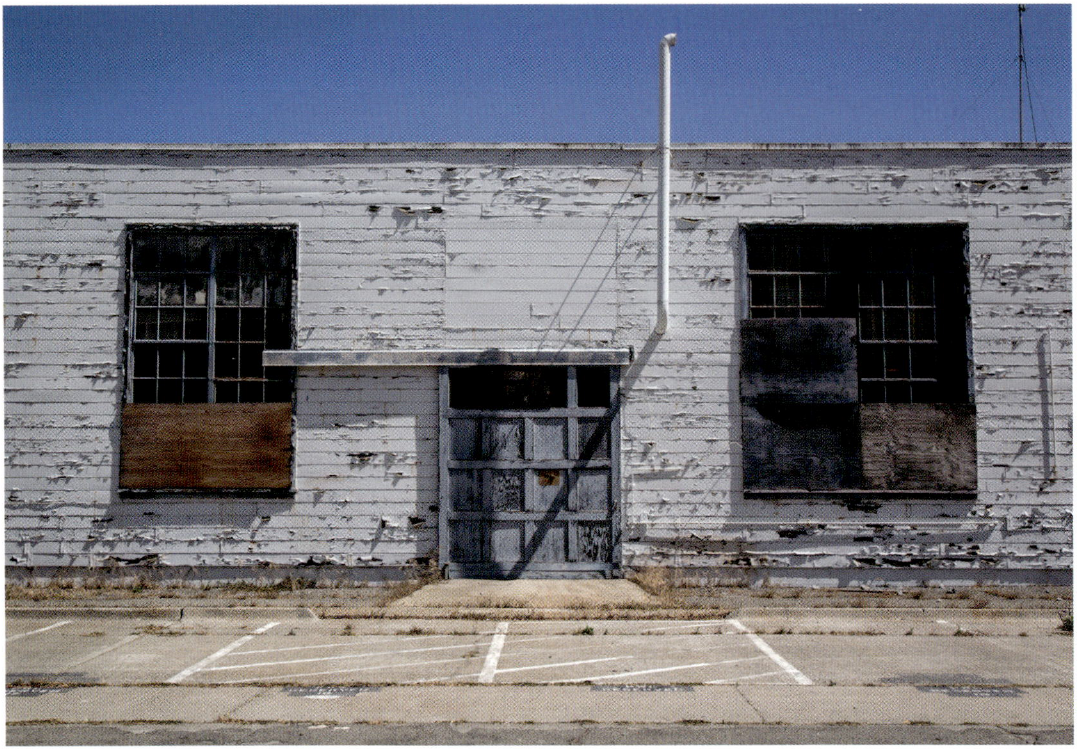

The front façade of an abandoned naval building.

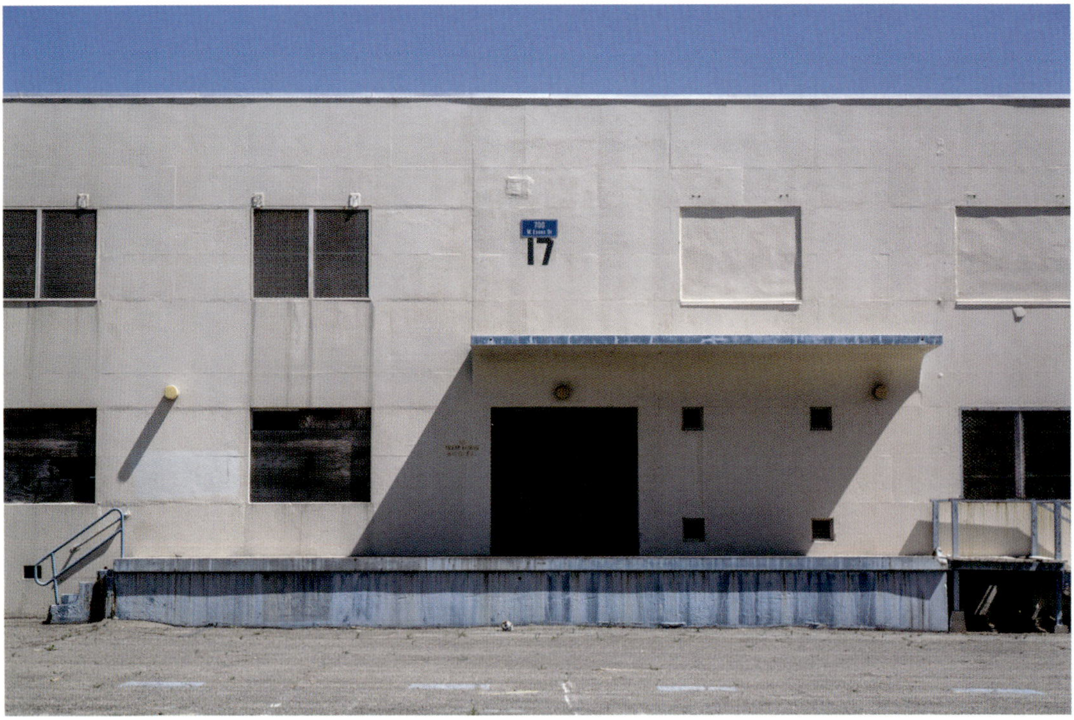

The buildings sprawl out over a massive complex in Alameda.

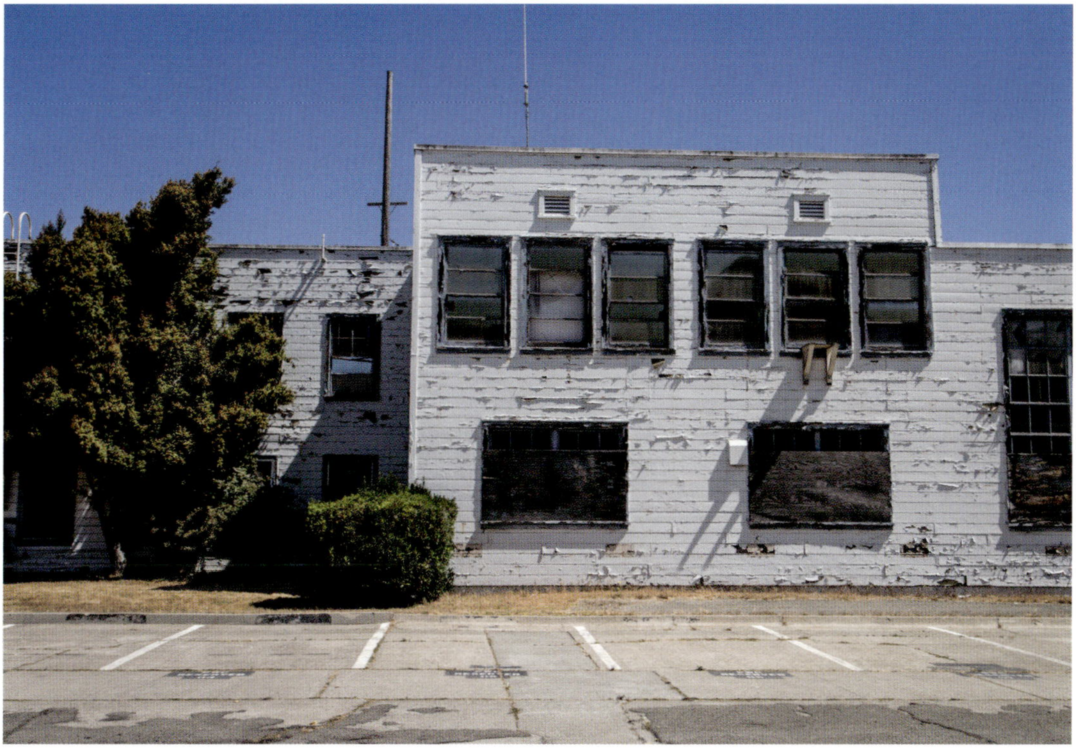

The Naval Base has not yet been repurposed for some other use.

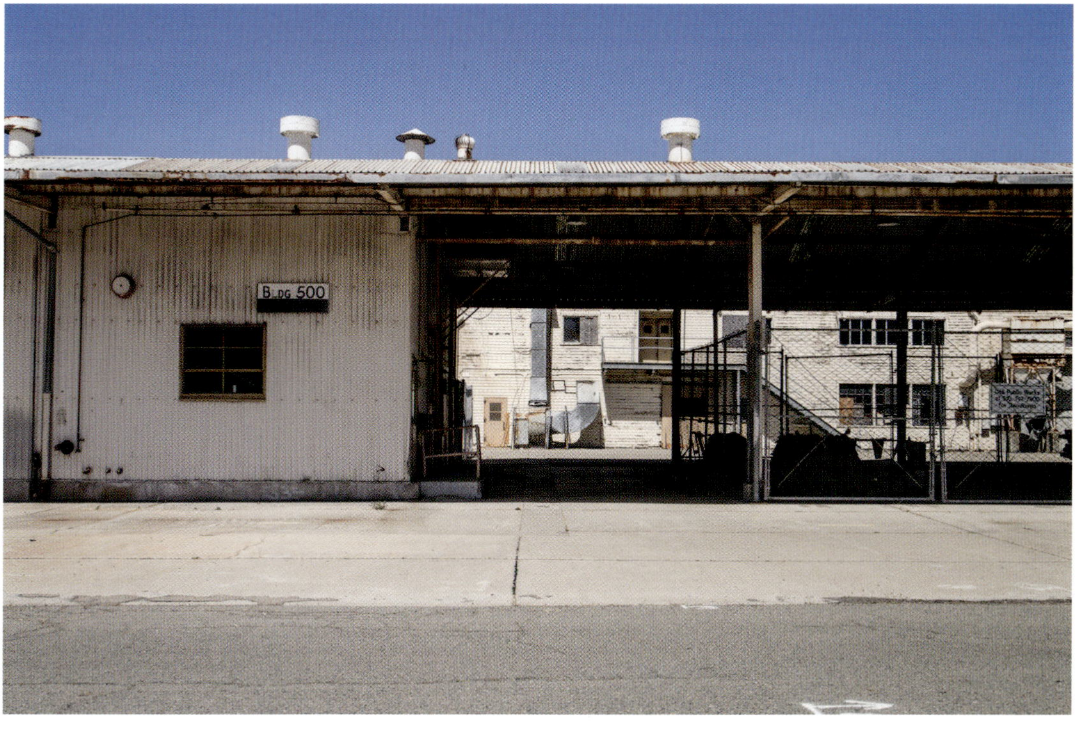

Building 500 at Alameda Naval Base.

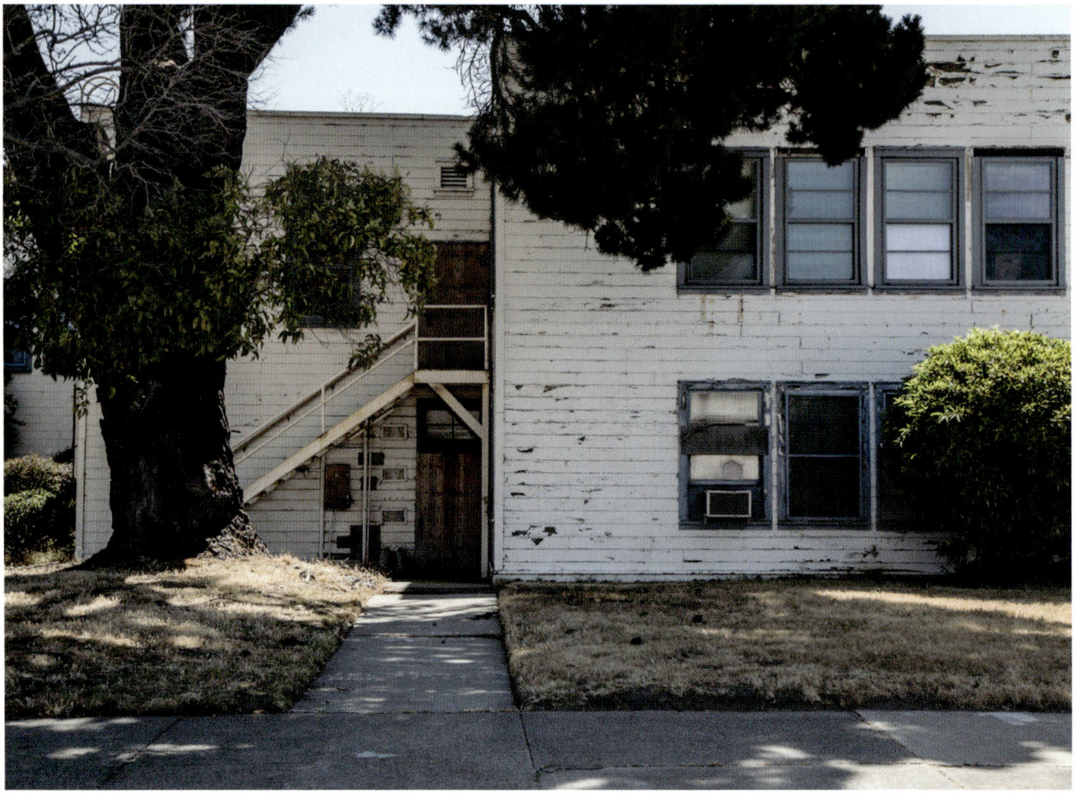

Most buildings at the Naval Base lie forgotten and unlabeled.

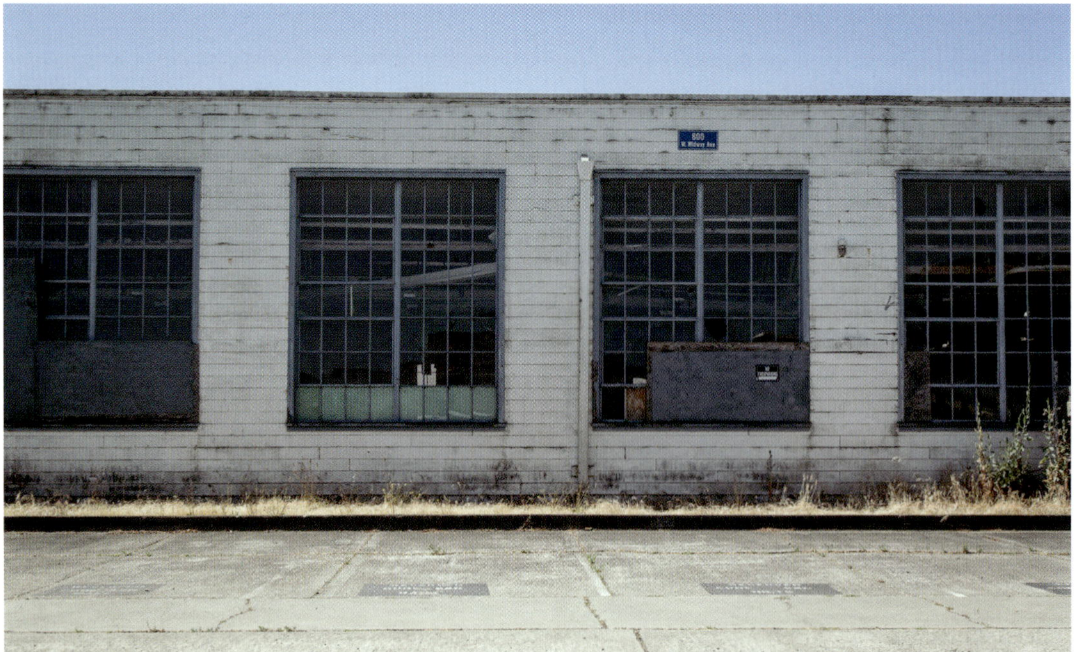

One of many abandoned buildings at Alameda Naval Base.

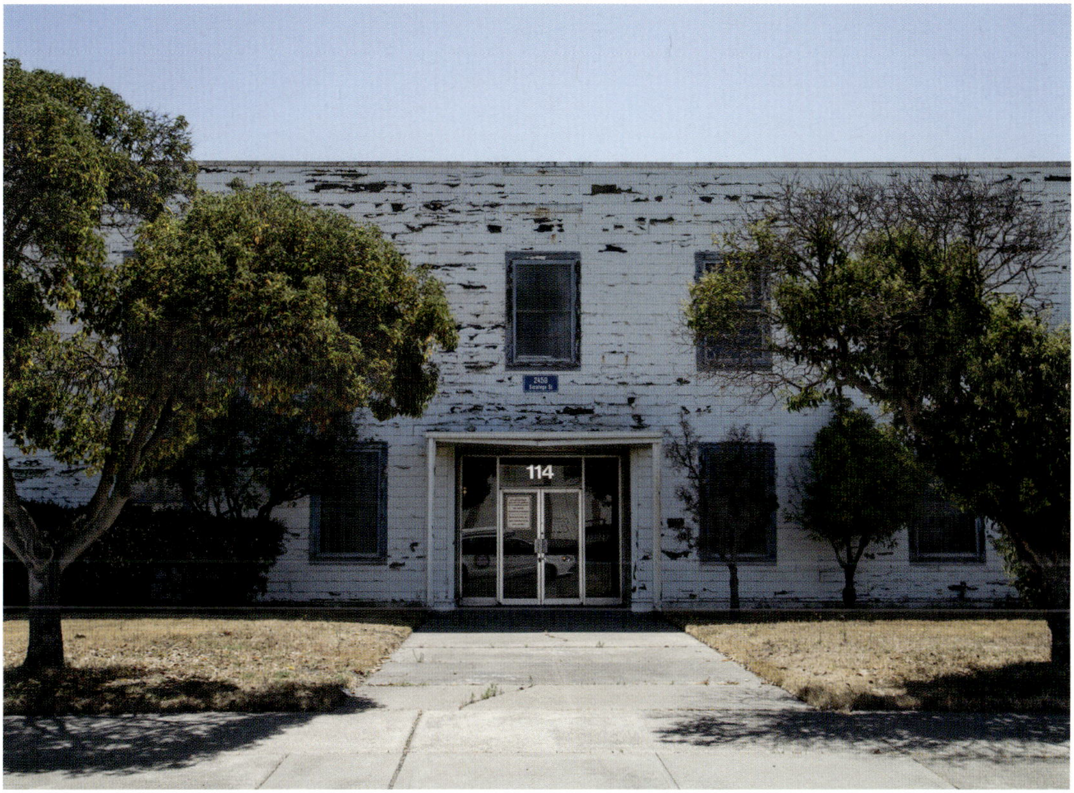

The entrance door to this abandoned Naval Base building looks almost new.

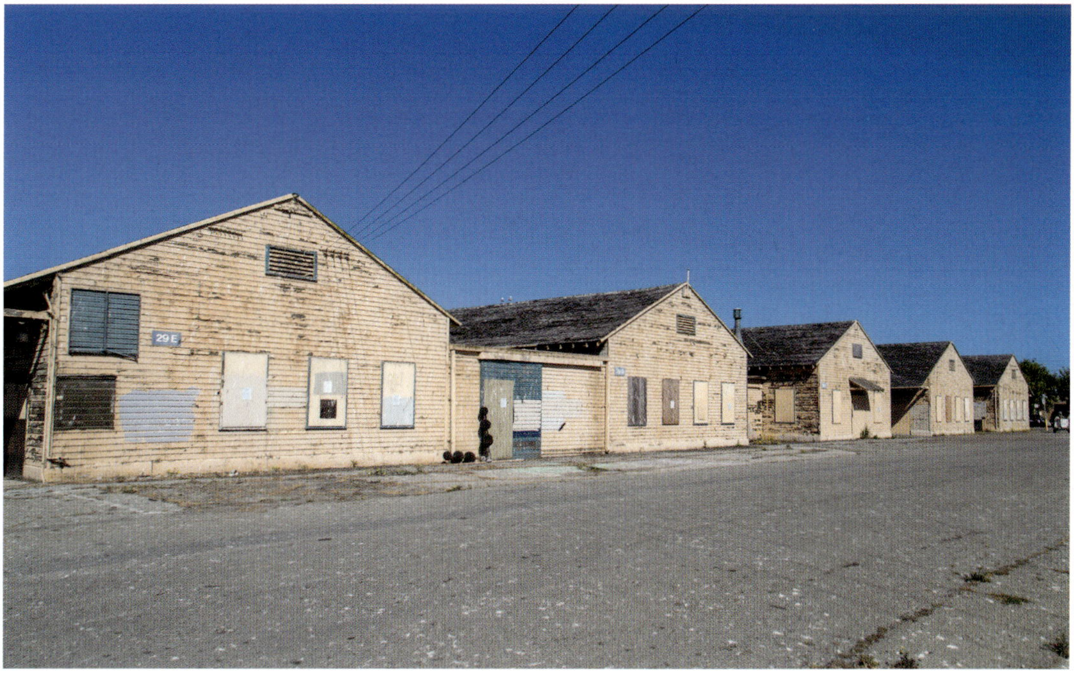

Barrack-looking buildings line the streets of the abandoned Naval Station Treasure Island.

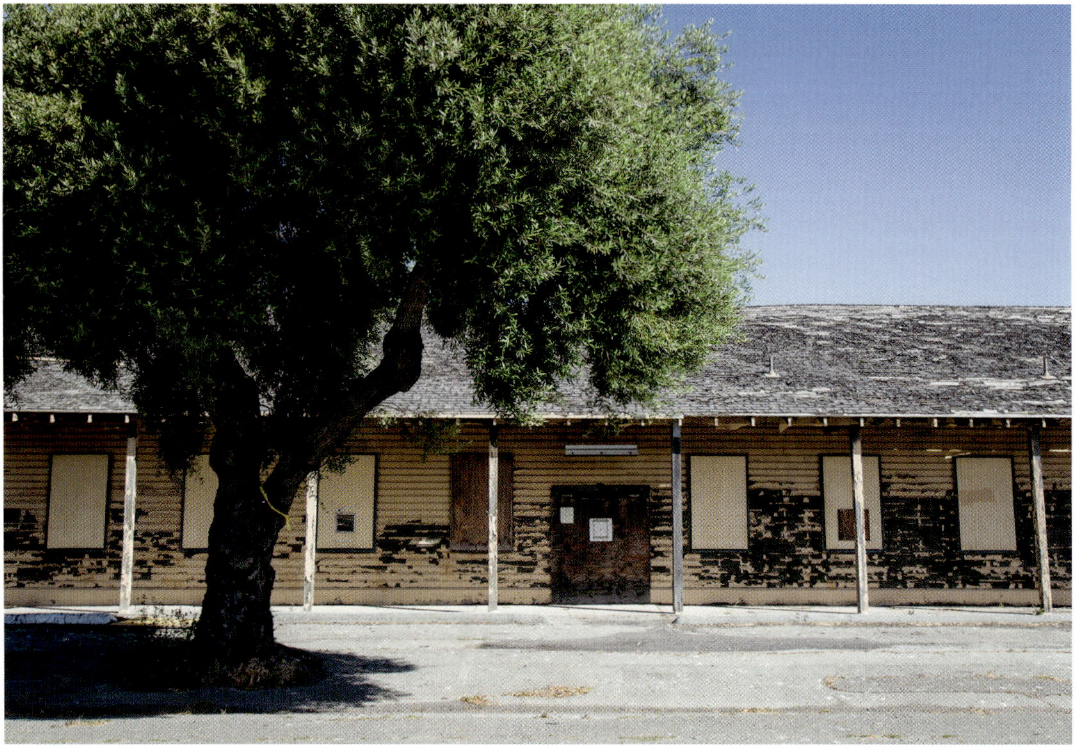

Many of the Naval Station buildings are unlabeled, and their purpose is uncertain.

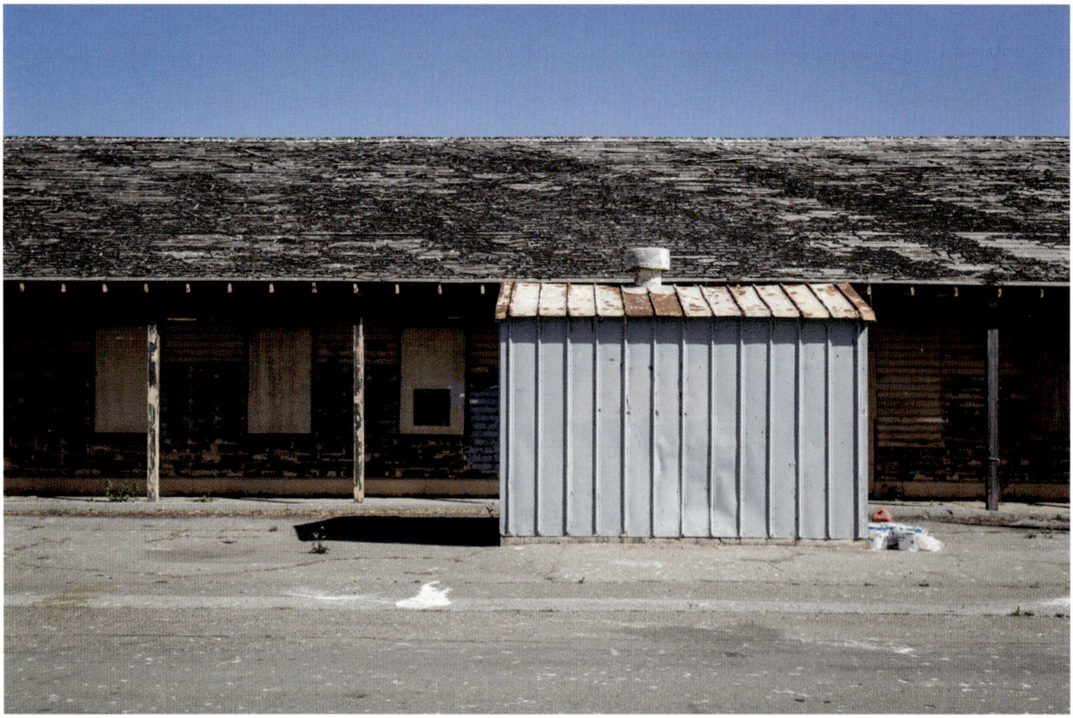

More abandoned naval station structures.

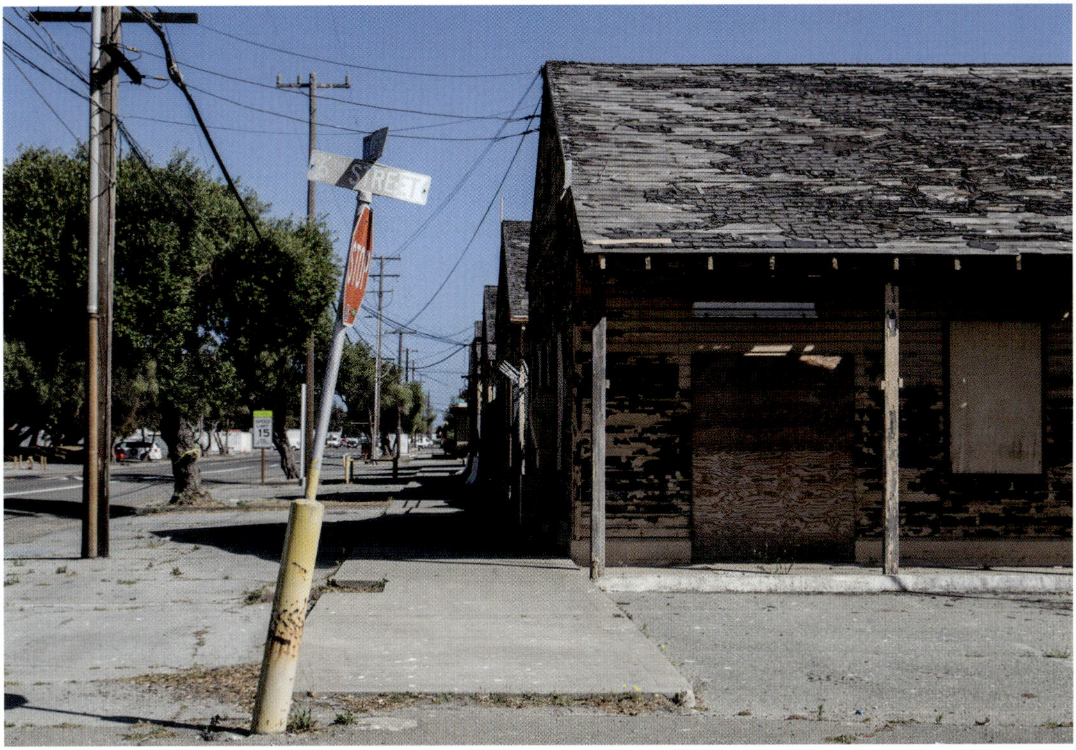

A sign sits falling and rusting on an old intersection at the station.

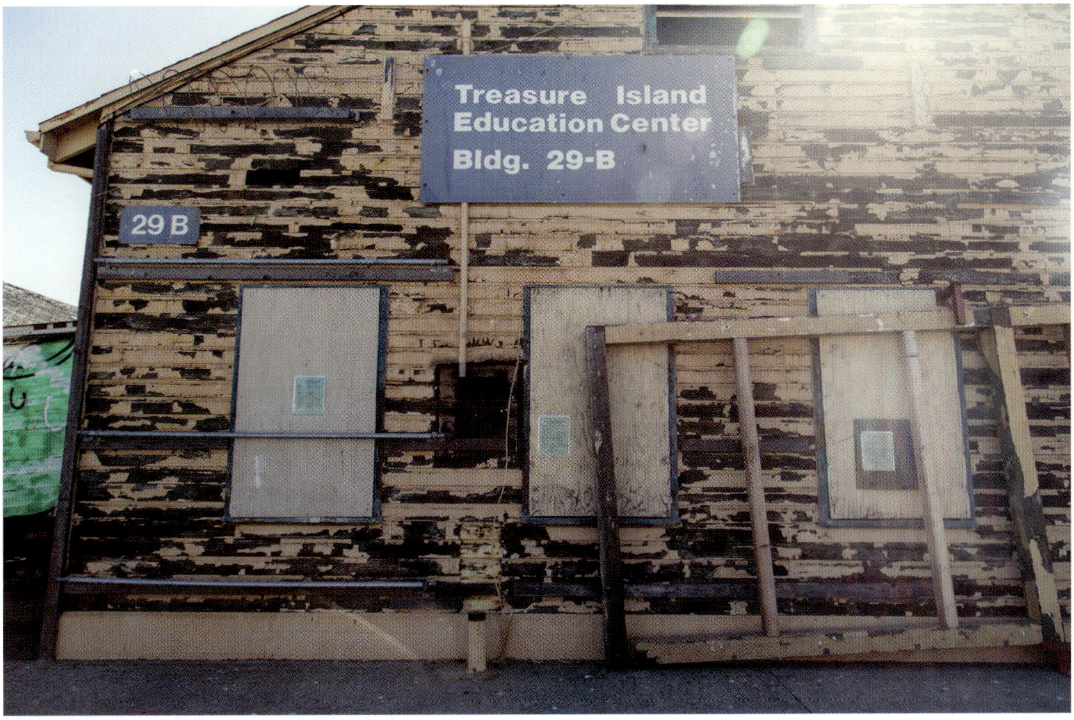

More educational buildings at Naval Station Treasure Island.

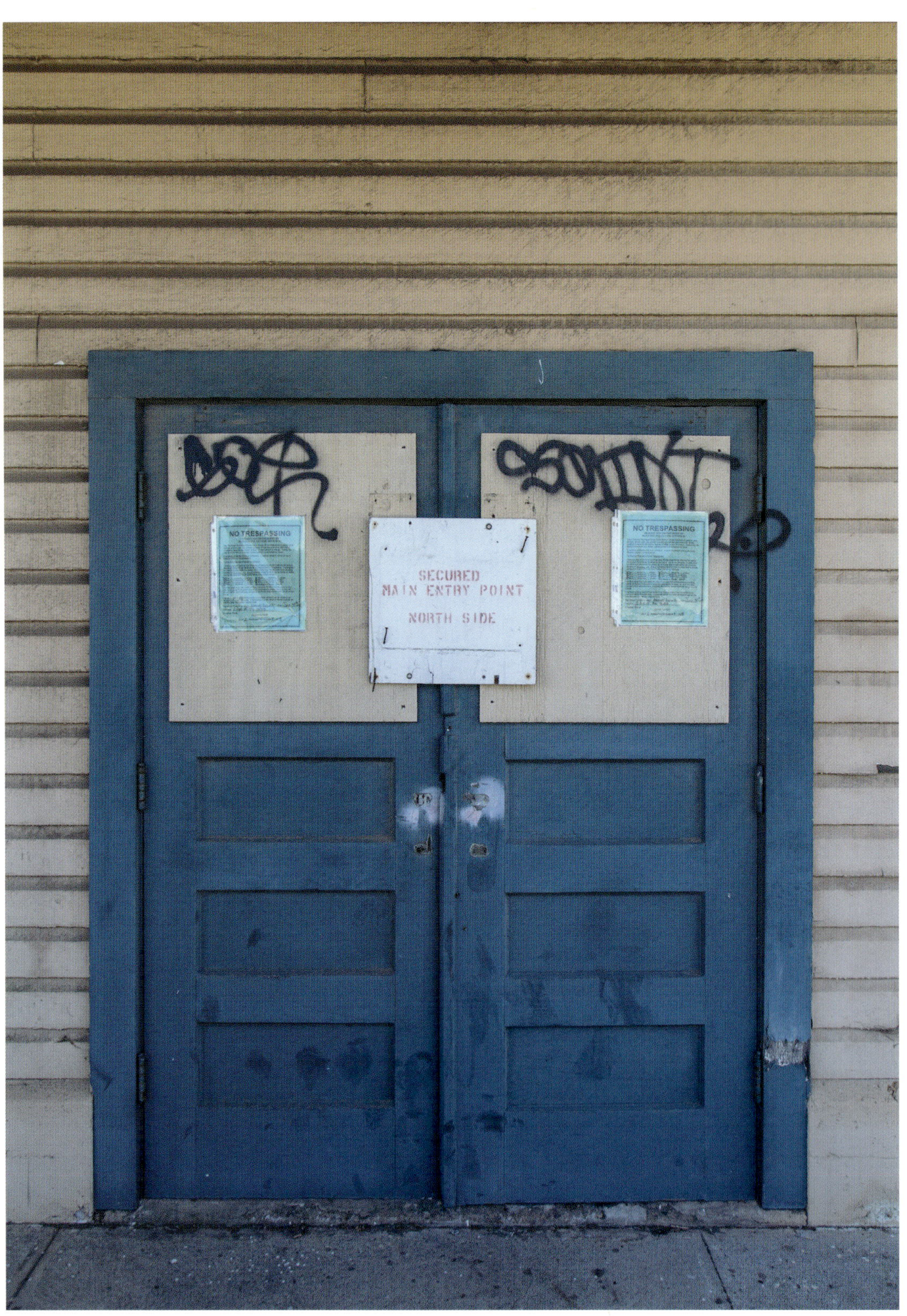

Brightly colored door in the abandoned Naval Station Treasure Island.

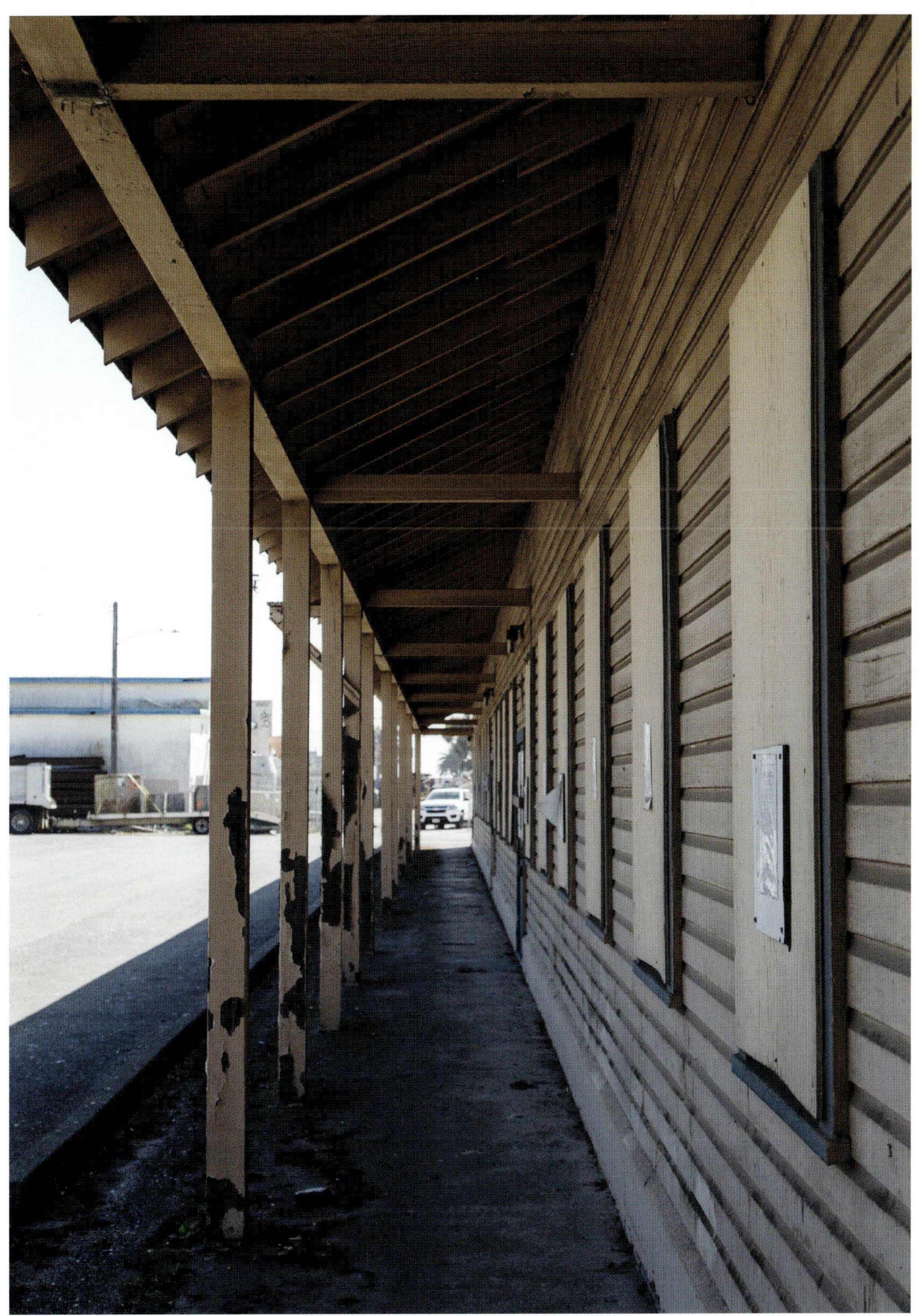

Former educational buildings on the island.

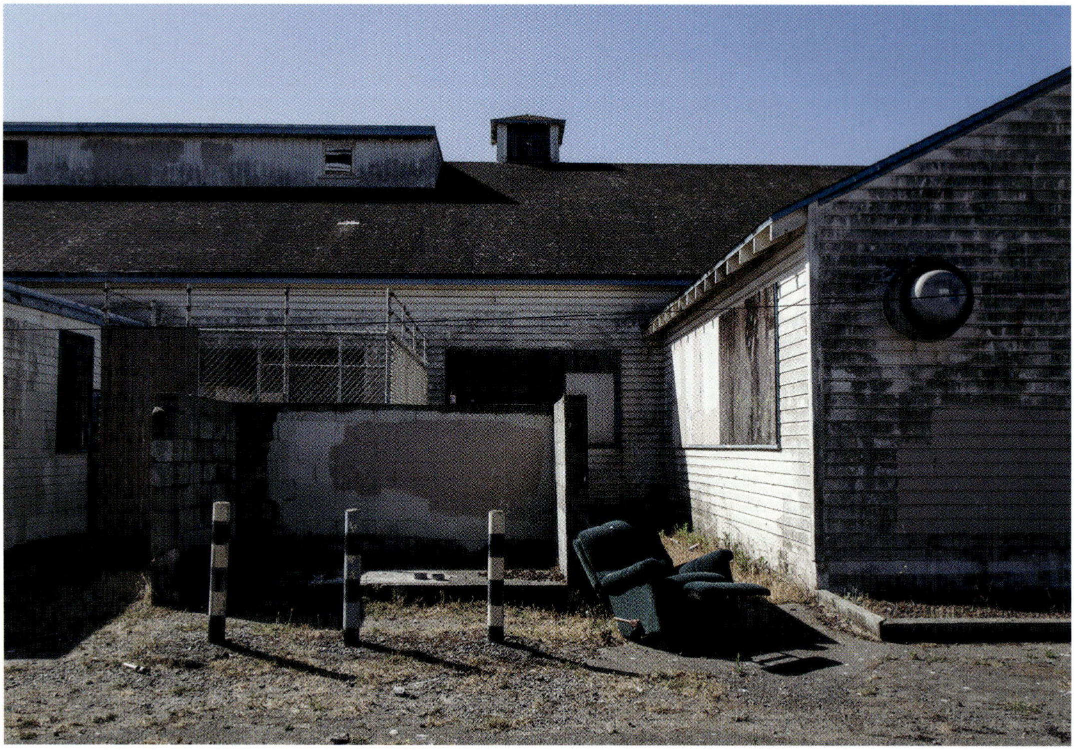

The naval station was recently abandoned, so many of the buildings are still fully standing.

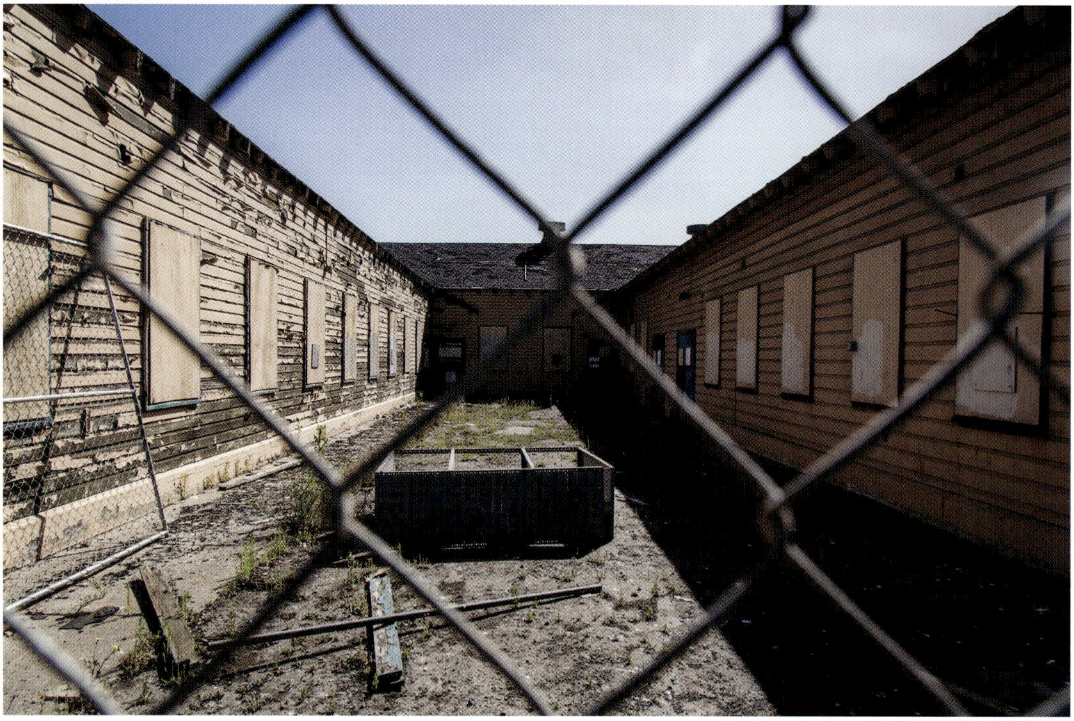

Looking through a chain link fence at the abandoned naval station.

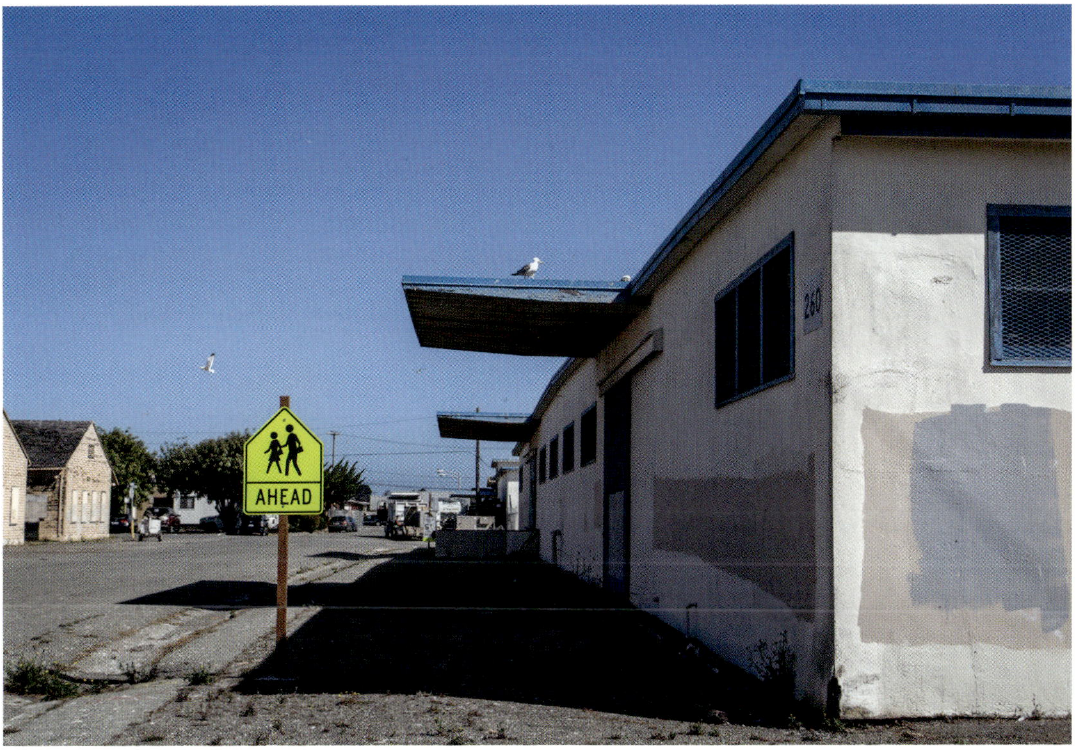

Signs warn of school crossings at the abandoned station.

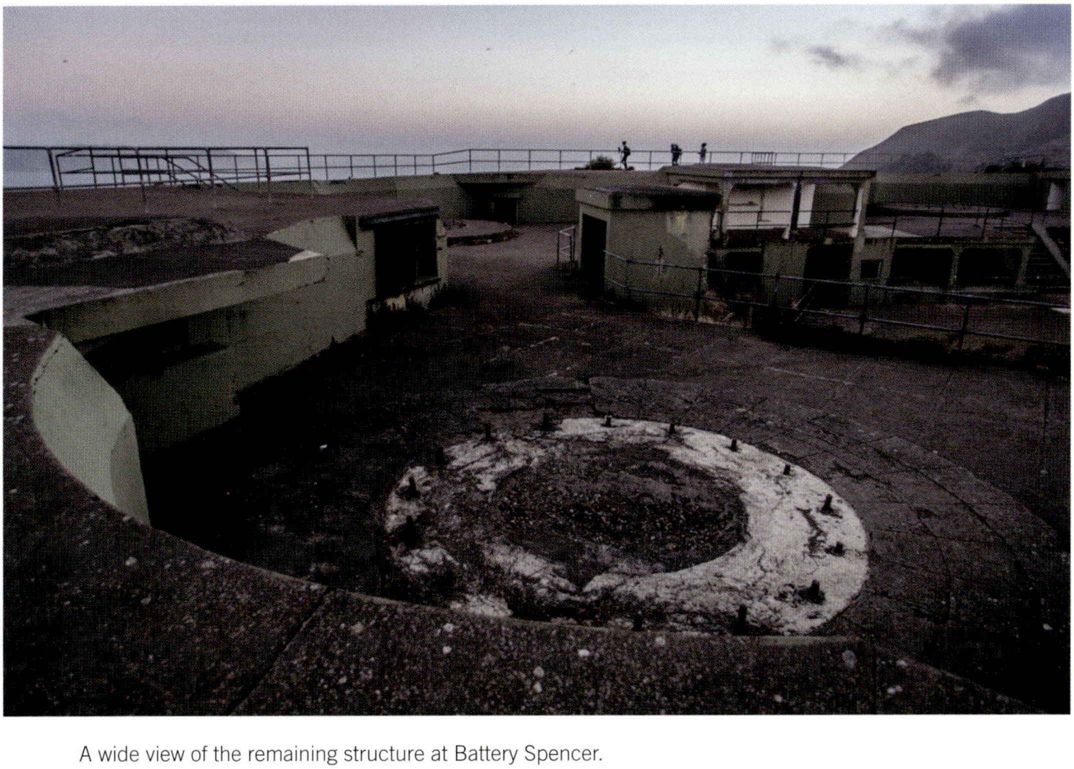

A wide view of the remaining structure at Battery Spencer.

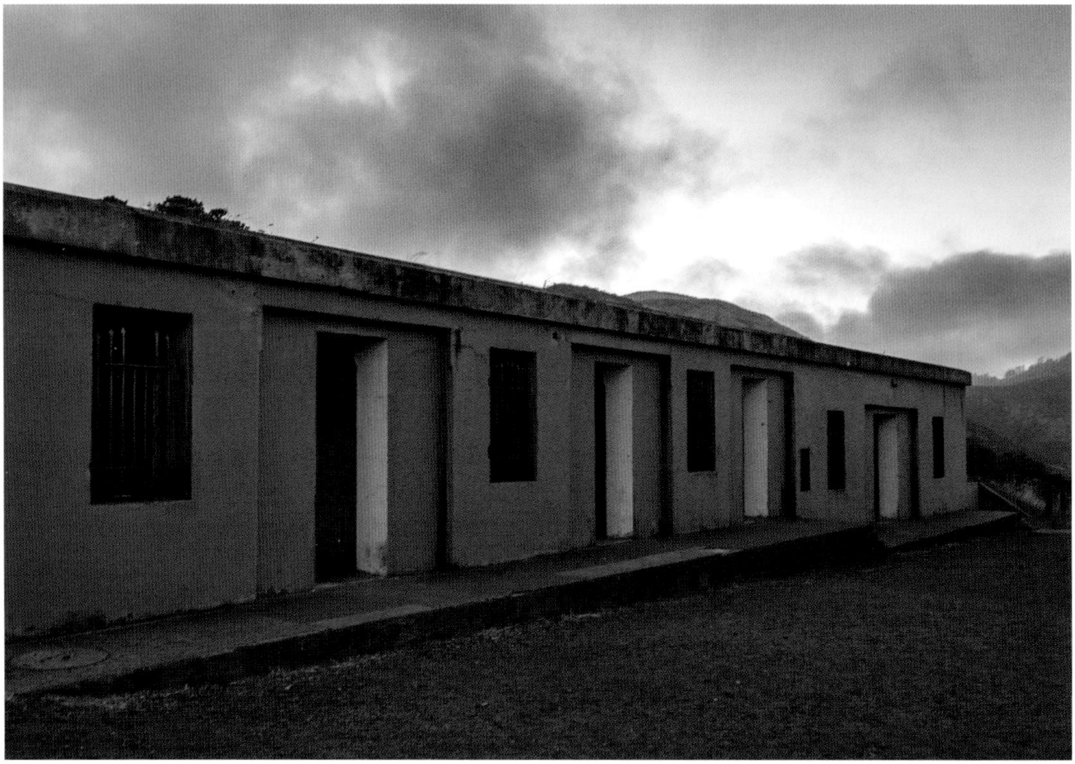

Structures for storage remain throughout Battery Spencer.

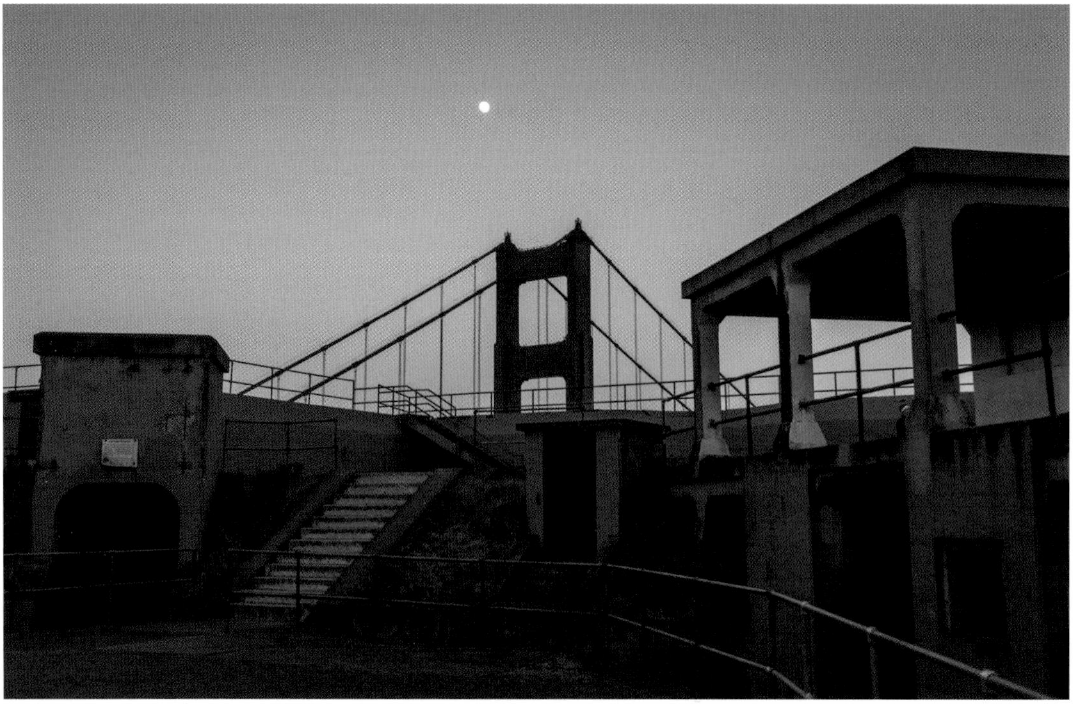

Battery Spencer has great views of the Golden Gate Bridge.

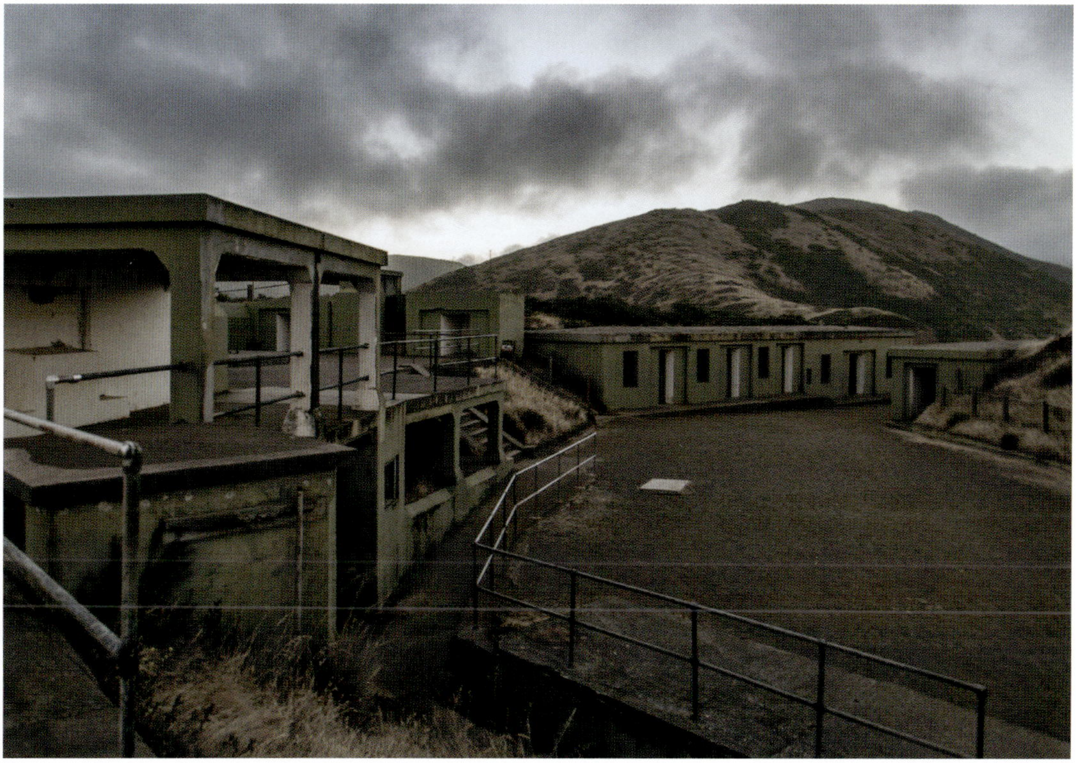

Battery Spencer is located against the backdrop of the beautiful Marin Headlands.

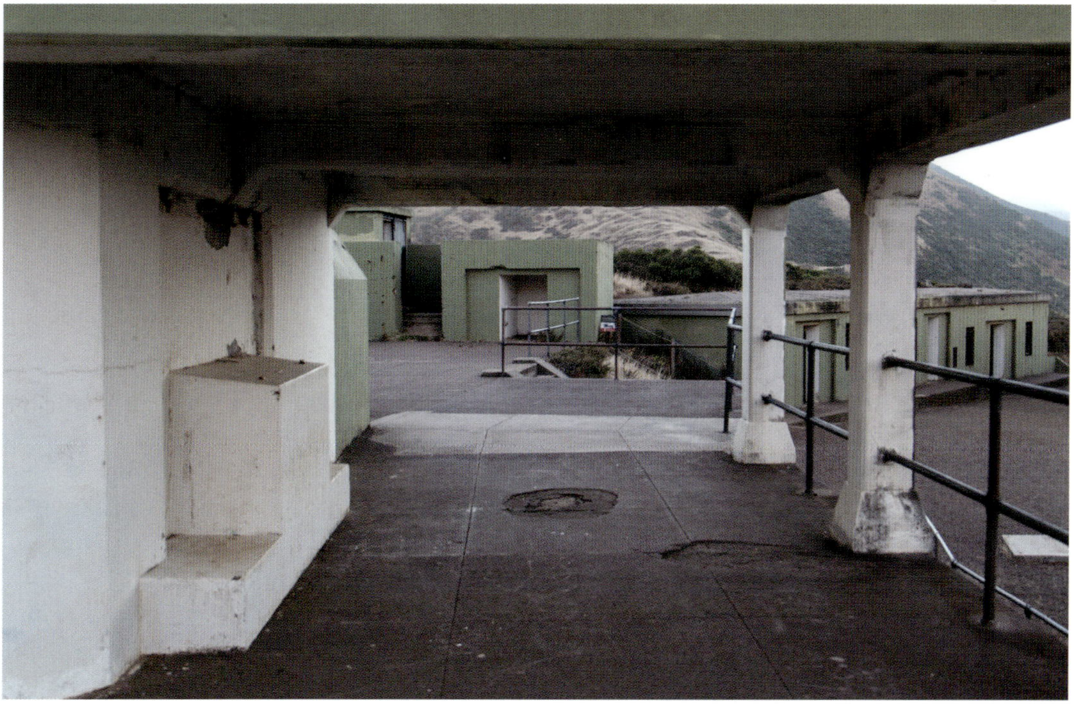

Walking through the former military structure.

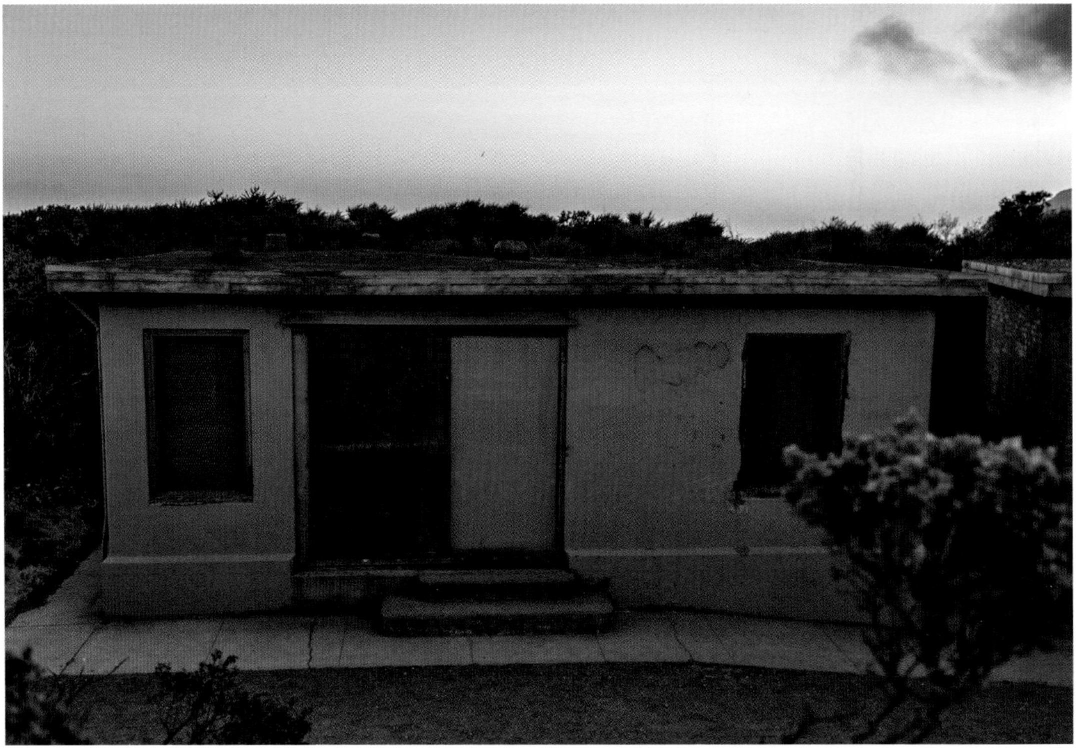

One of the remaining Battery Spencer structures.

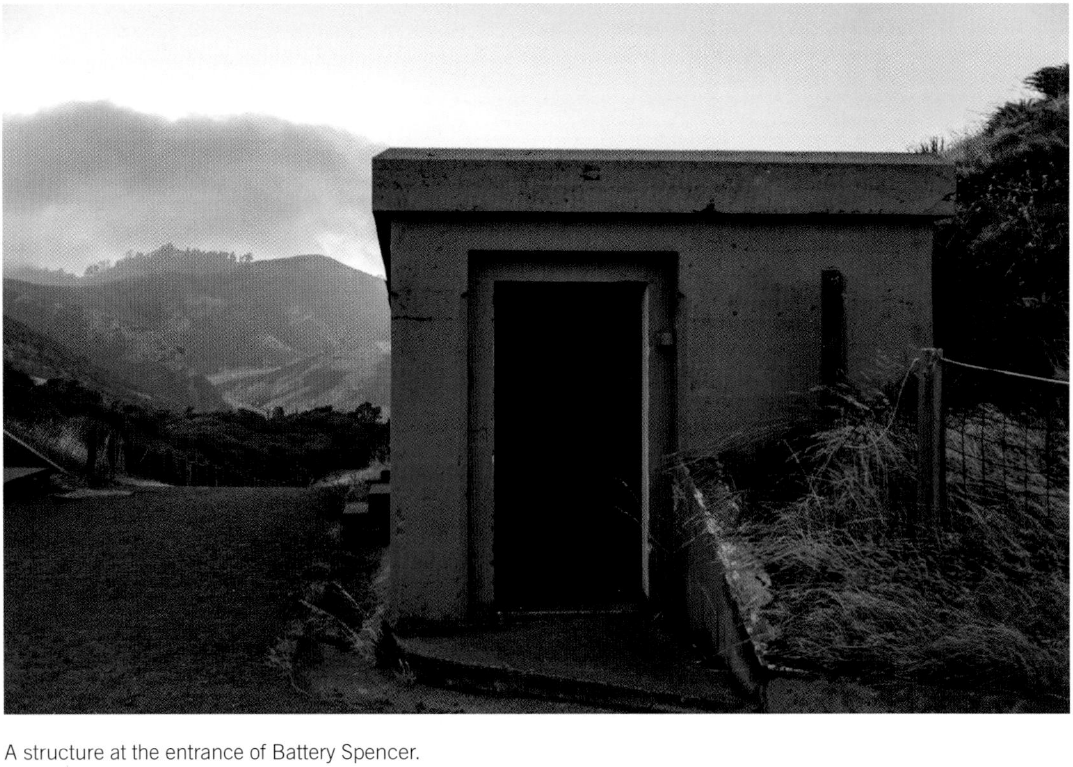

A structure at the entrance of Battery Spencer.

6

ABANDONED ODDITIES IN NORTHERN CALIFORNIA

POINT REYES SHIPWRECK

A small fishing boat ran aground on Tomales Bay some years ago, and now remains a cool local attraction for travelers and photographers. That description is pretty much all the information that exists regarding the mysterious small wreck outside Inverness with "Point Reyes" painted on its side.

Regardless of its origin, there's no denying the scenic beauty of this abandoned boat on the central California coast. Located behind a grocery store in a small seaside town, the Point Reyes shipwreck (or more accurately, boat-wreck), sits perched on a sandbar, often shrouded in the area's usual clouds and fog.

The boat on Point Reyes may be a relatively minor wreck, but it still serves as a reminder of the rough seas local sailors have had to navigate, and major wrecks that have happened in the same area. The narrow waterway leading to San Francisco is also frequently shrouded in fog, causing sometimes-fatal wrecks, such as the destruction of a 380-foot cargo steamship named the SS *Selja*, which sunk to the bottom of the bay in November of 1910.

Depending on the tide and the time of year, the Point Reyes boat is sometimes completely inaccessible due to high water. However, visitors should avoid entering the boat even if they can access it, as the rotted wood is full of holes and can easily give way.

J'S AMUSEMENT PARK

Located outside the rural forest town of Guerneville, California, J's Amusement Park seems completely out of place at first glance. Visitors may wonder why anyone would

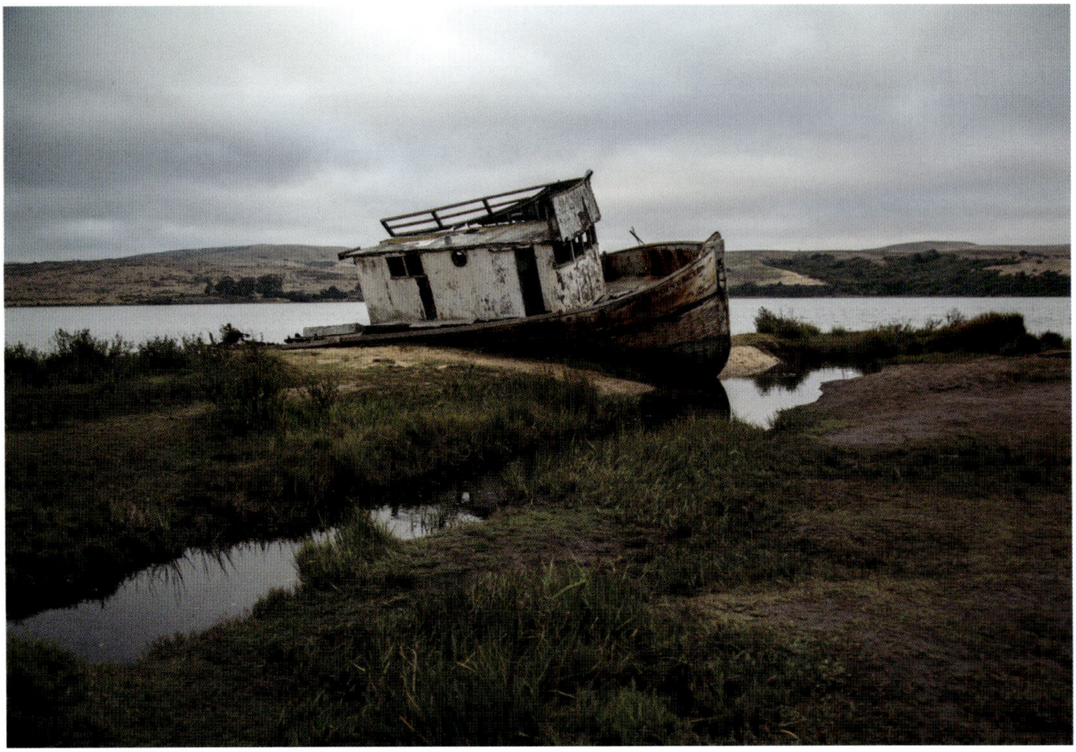

The shipwreck ran aground years ago, though no one knows exactly how.

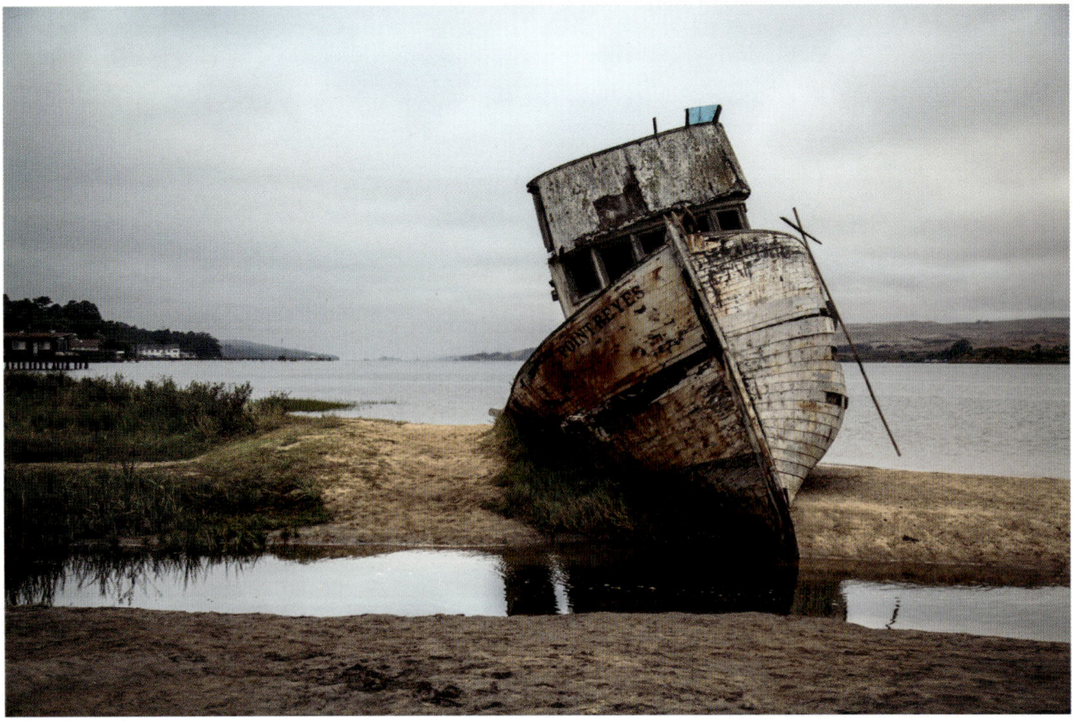

A front view of the shipwreck.

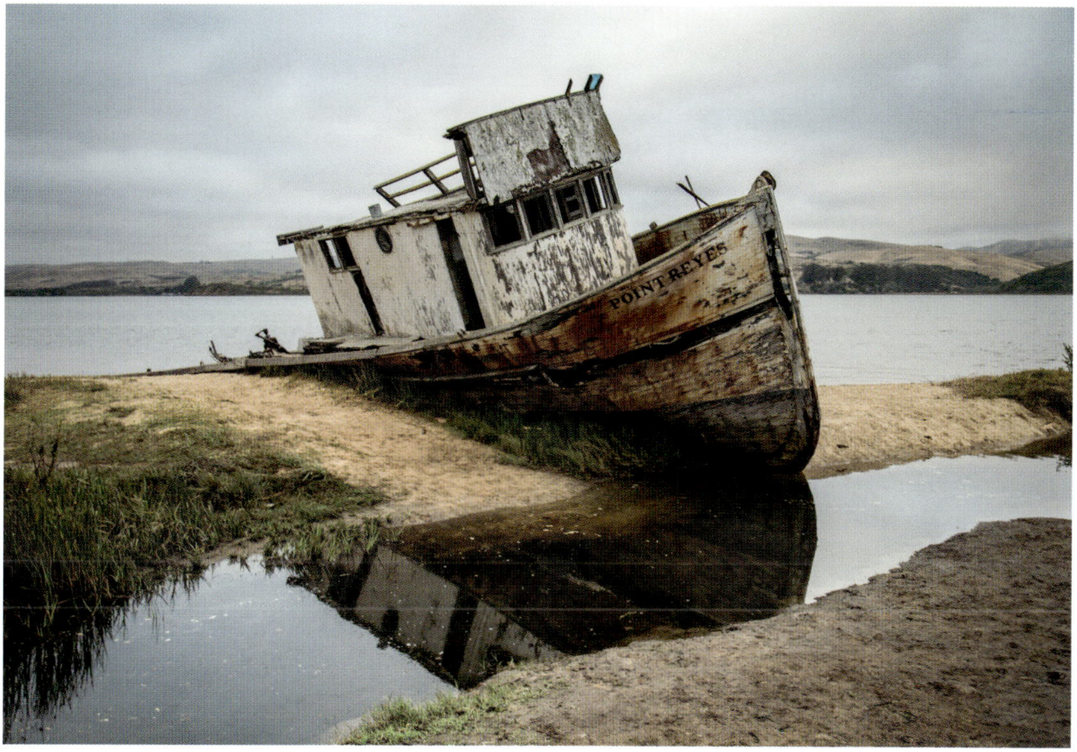

Reflections of the Point Reyes wreck in the water underneath.

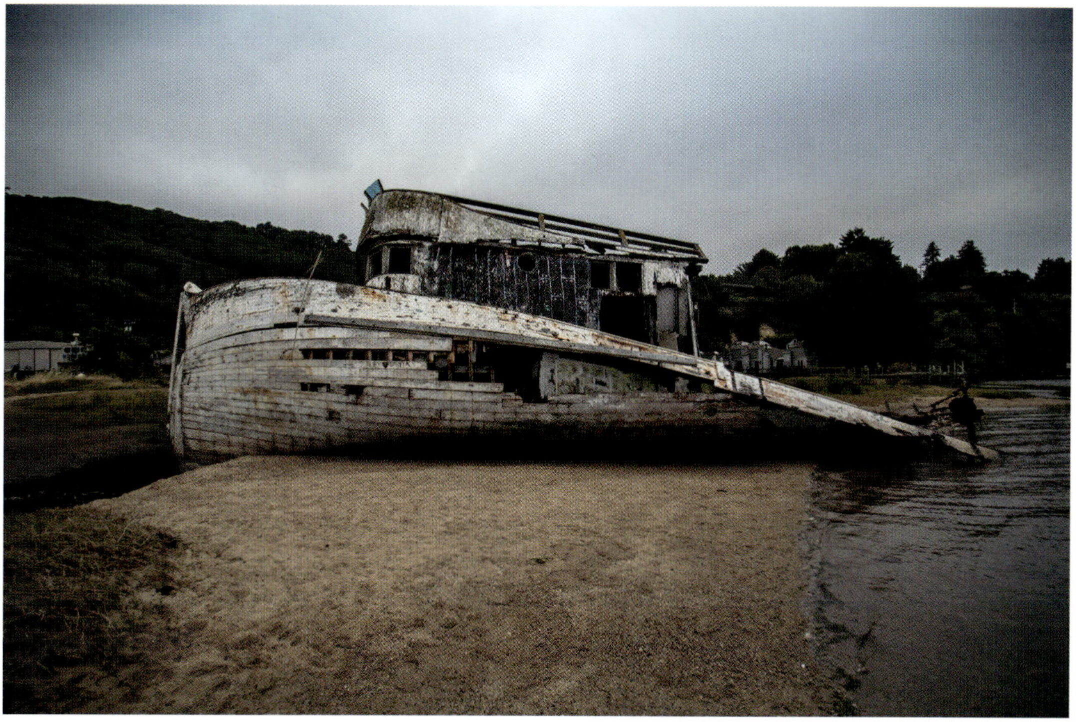

The other side of the shipwreck, damaged by fire years after the wreck.

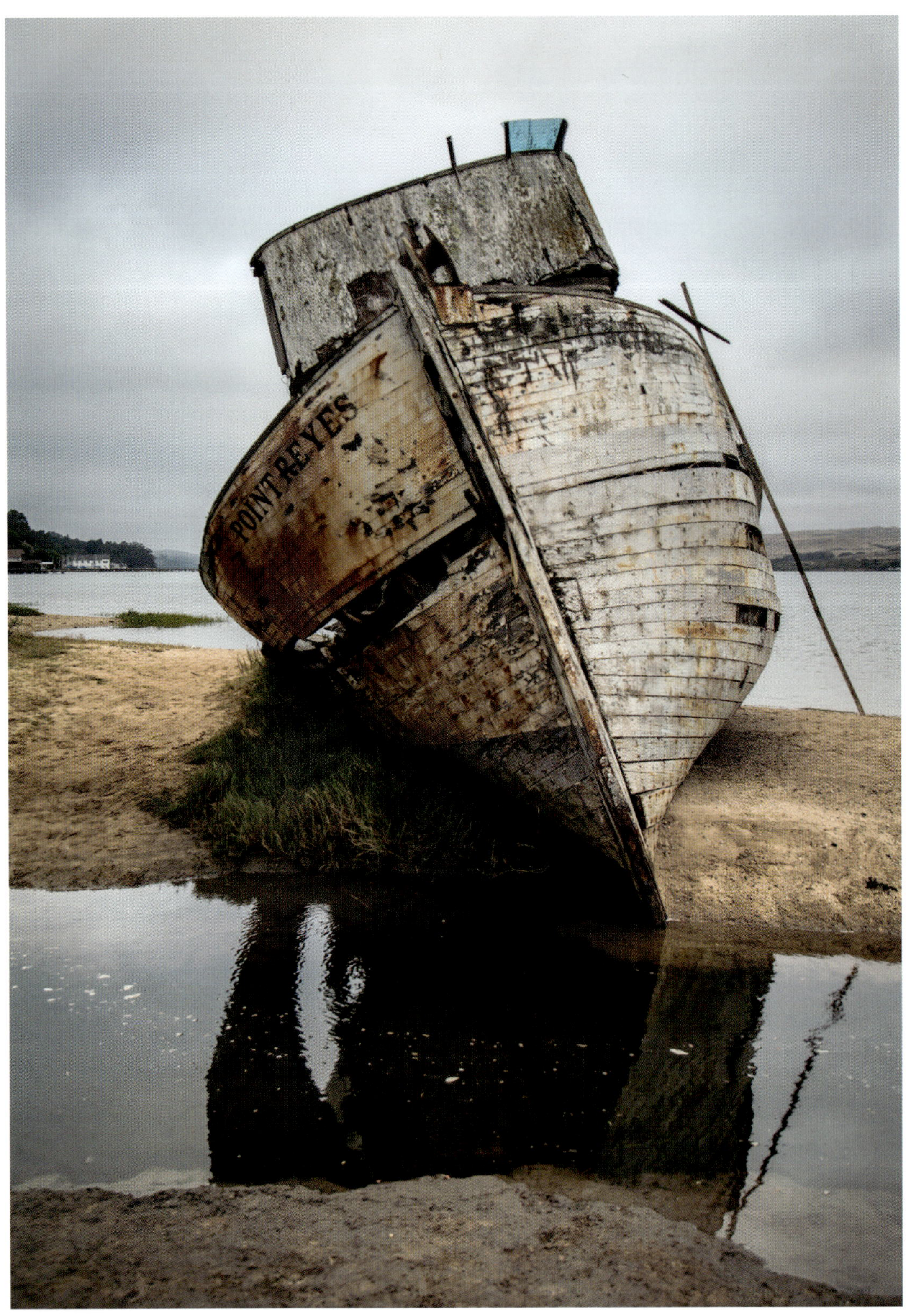

Reflection of the Point Reyes Shipwreck.

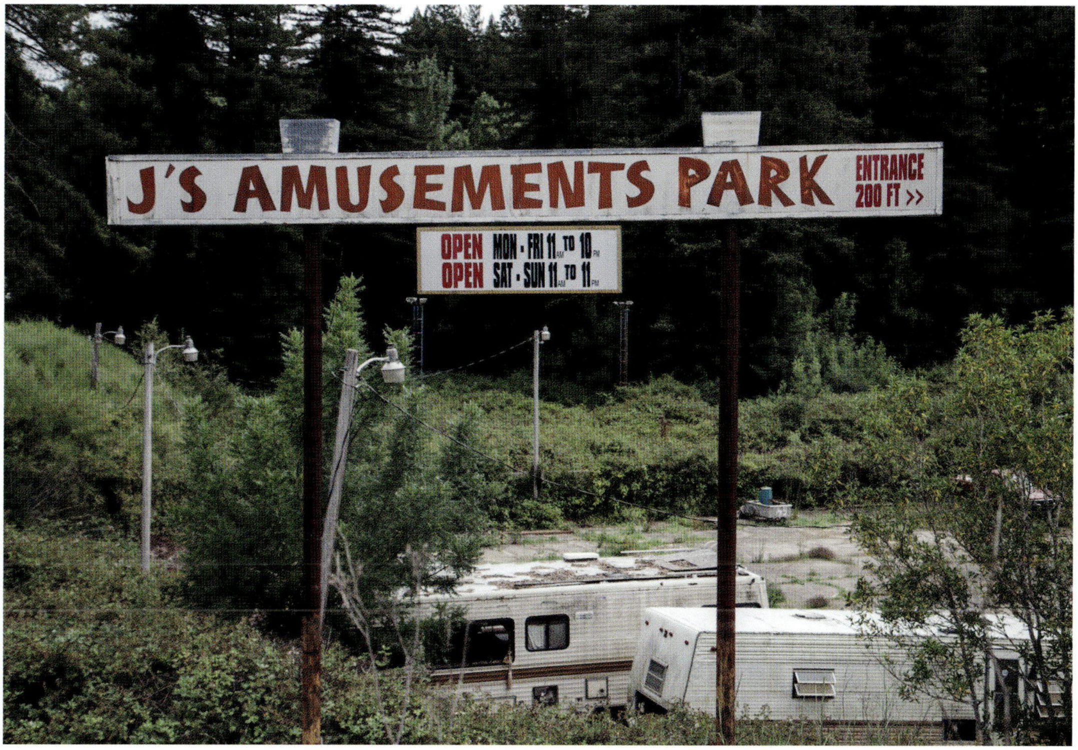

A sign by a little-used road indicates that J's Amusement Park was here.

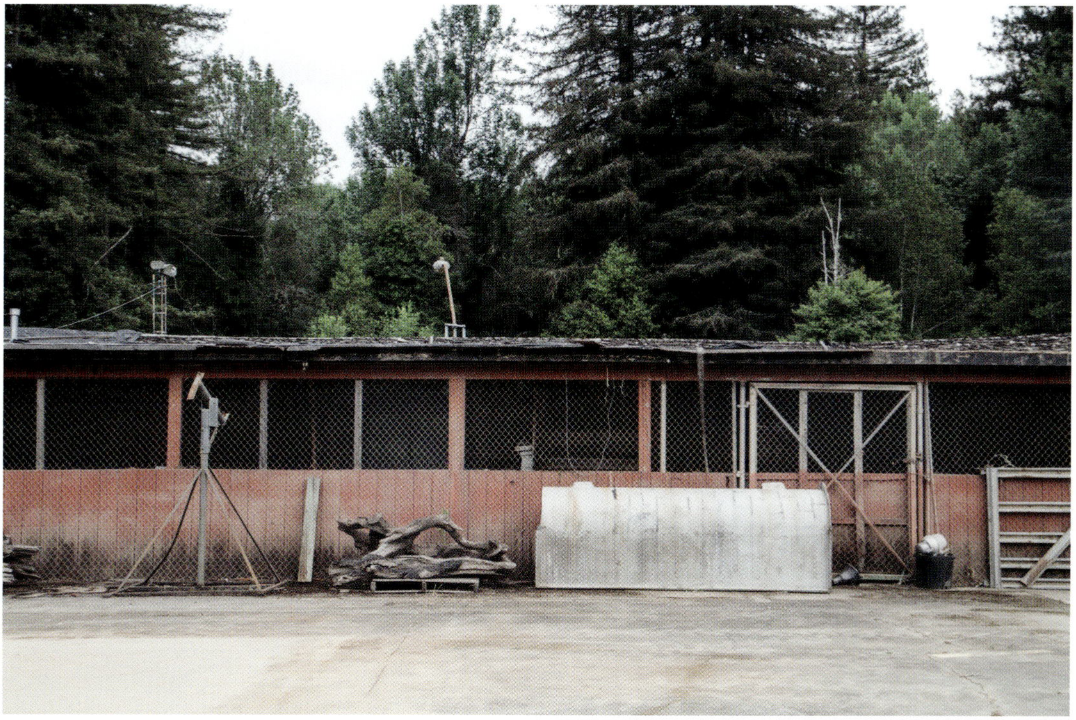

One of the few remaining buildings at the old amusement park.

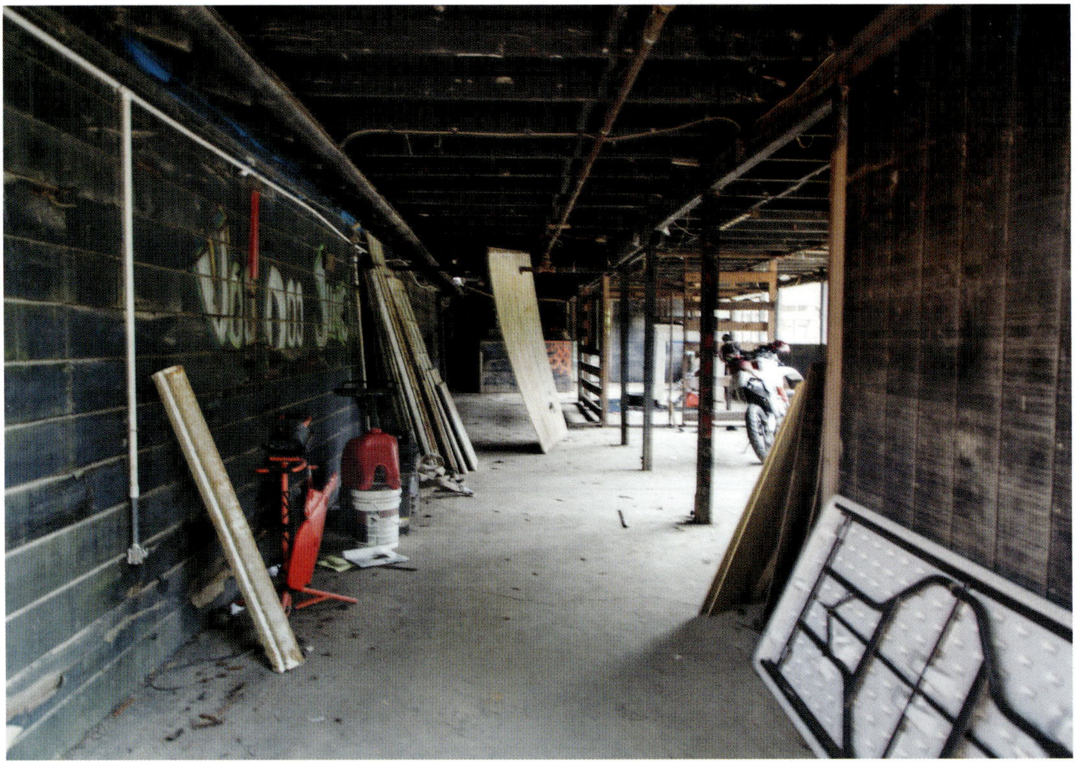

Garage and storage from the amusement park.

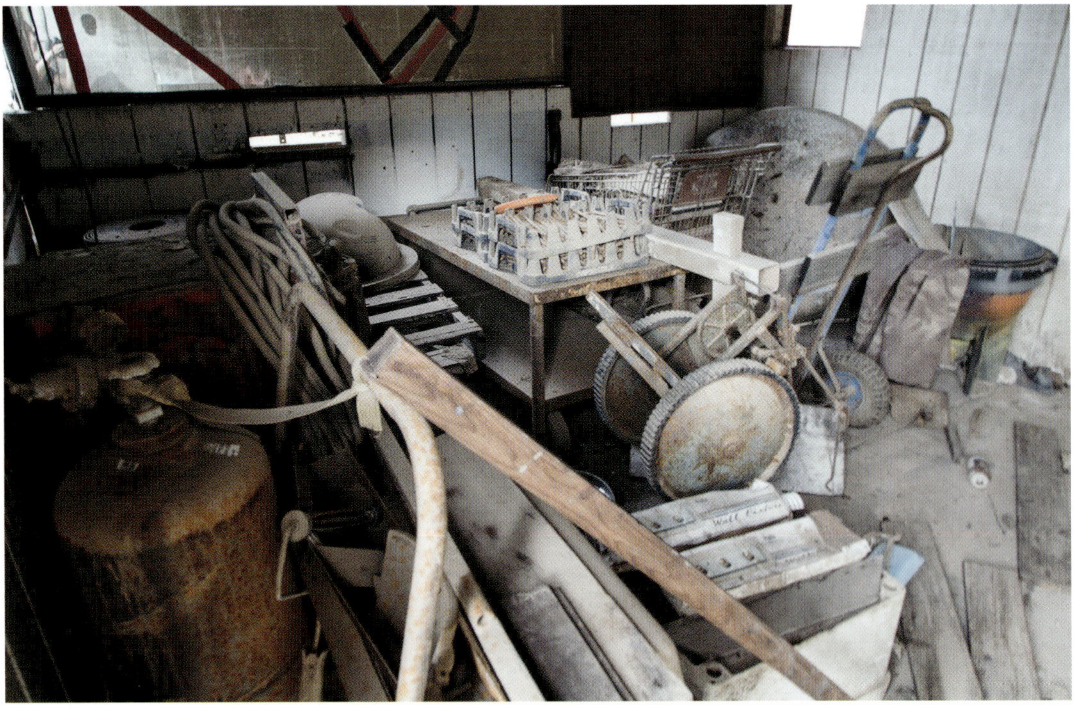

Leftover storage space.

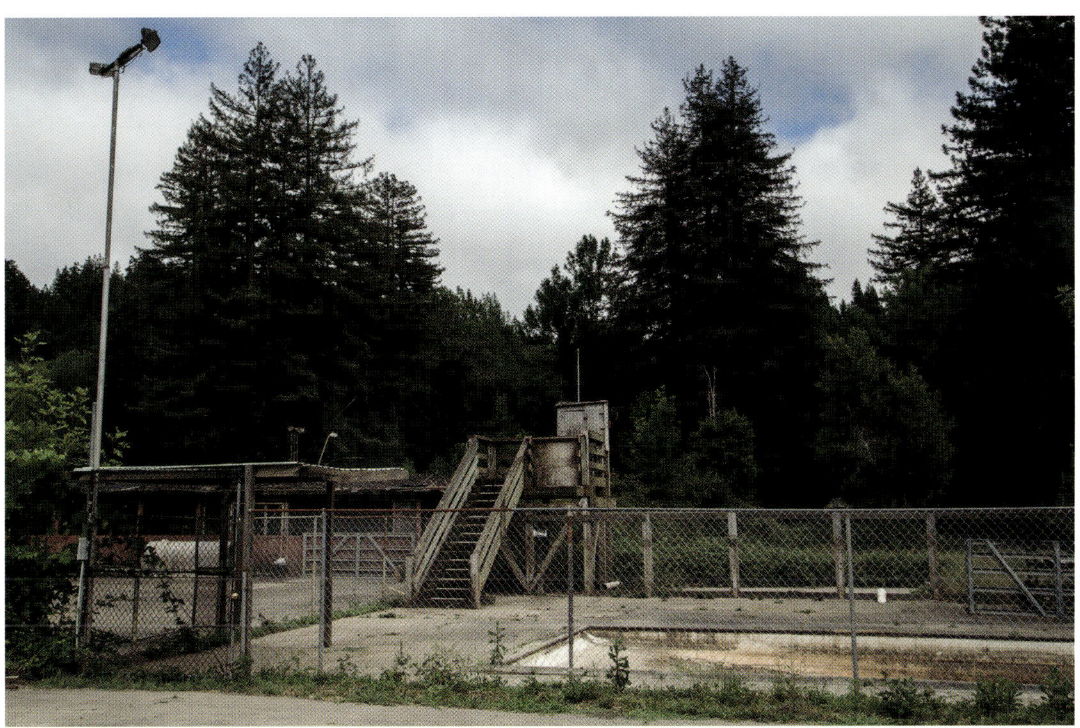

An abandoned pool and play area.

even think to set up an amusement park in the first place in such an out-of-the-way location, surrounded by a towering forest and miniscule towns.

However, this small park operated for over four decades after being founded by the Skaggs family, drawing in locals and visiting families from miles around. J's Amusement Park expanded to the point where it featured a roller coaster, racetrack, and house of horrors.

Unfortunately, in 2003, J's had to shut down due to rising costs. For a few years after the amusement park closed, the grounds were converted to a seasonal campground, used mostly by outside visitors coming to locally famous Guerneville events.

Now, the campground is largely abandoned, and many of J's Amusement Park's more iconic structures have fallen into disrepair. However, curious visitors can still look around some abandoned ruins that remain, including a pool.

THE TRAGEDY OF NEVADA COUNTY HOSPITAL

Though no abandoned hospital or sanatorium I can think of looks inviting, the exterior of Nevada County Hospital seems especially disturbing. Located in a rural residential area of Nevada City, the hospital's tragic past appears ingrained in the very structure itself.

Originally established relatively early in the US era of California's history, all the way back in 1860, Nevada County Hospital was used for many purposes over the years, from housing the mentally disturbed to low-risk inmates, before being decommissioned and abandoned in 2005. Its latest incarnation before being abandoned was as the Health Education and Welfare (HEW) Building.

Part of what led to the shutting down of the HEW facility was a tragic incident in 2001 that ended up causing state-wide legal change. That year, a mentally-ill man named Scott Thorpe, who had previously been treated at the HEW facility and believed it was poisoning him, became angry after being unable to see his psychiatrist. He then shot three people on the hospital grounds, killing two. Thorpe continued his spree at a nearby restaurant where he claimed one more life.

One of his victims at the hospital was nineteen-year-old Laura Wilcox. Her family was outraged that treatment had not been mandated for Thorpe, who was considered severely mentally ill.

Shortly after the shooting and the family's legal fight to change the system, Laura's Law was passed in 2003, which enabled counties and judges to court order outpatient treatment for mentally ill people who fit certain criteria, including possibly presenting a danger to others.

Walking through the hospital grounds in the present day, the incident seems to have irreversibly stained the very atmosphere of the building. Previous visitors have plastered graffiti on the exterior walls, pointing to the doors of the hospital and claiming there are ghosts inside. From left-behind clothes and notebooks, it is also clear a couple of people have made the hospital grounds their unofficial home. The contrast between the charming courtyard and now-faded colorful murals that adorn the hospital, and the eerie, cracked, broken façade, is a sight to behold.

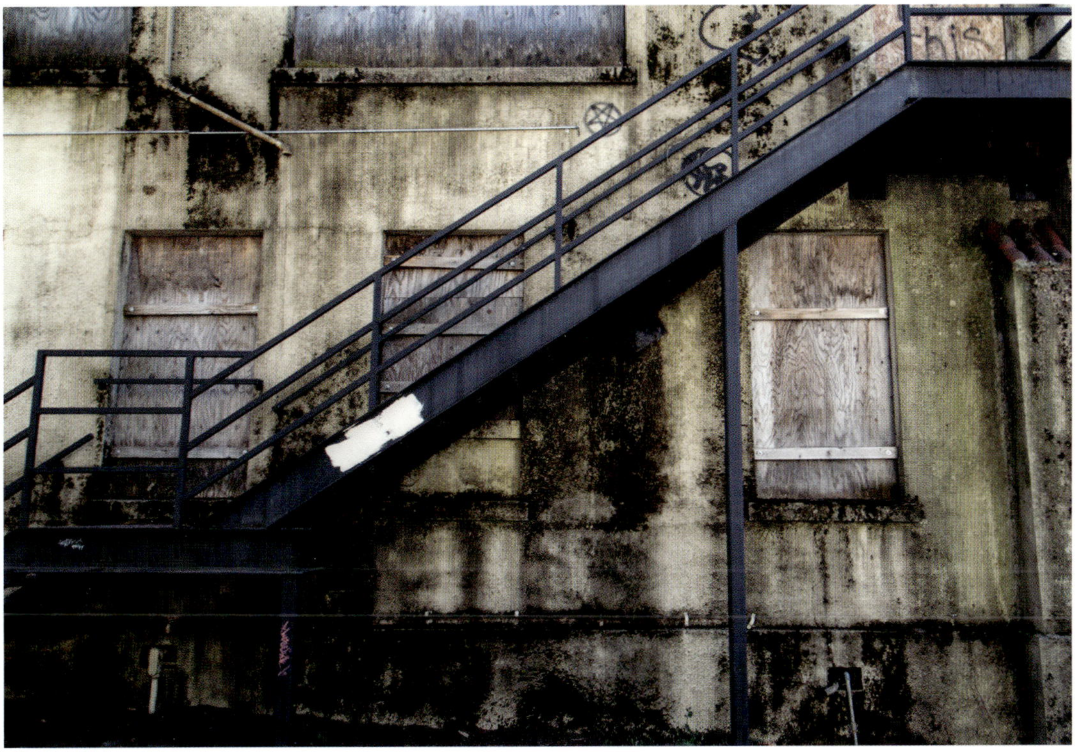

Exterior hospital stairways rust over.

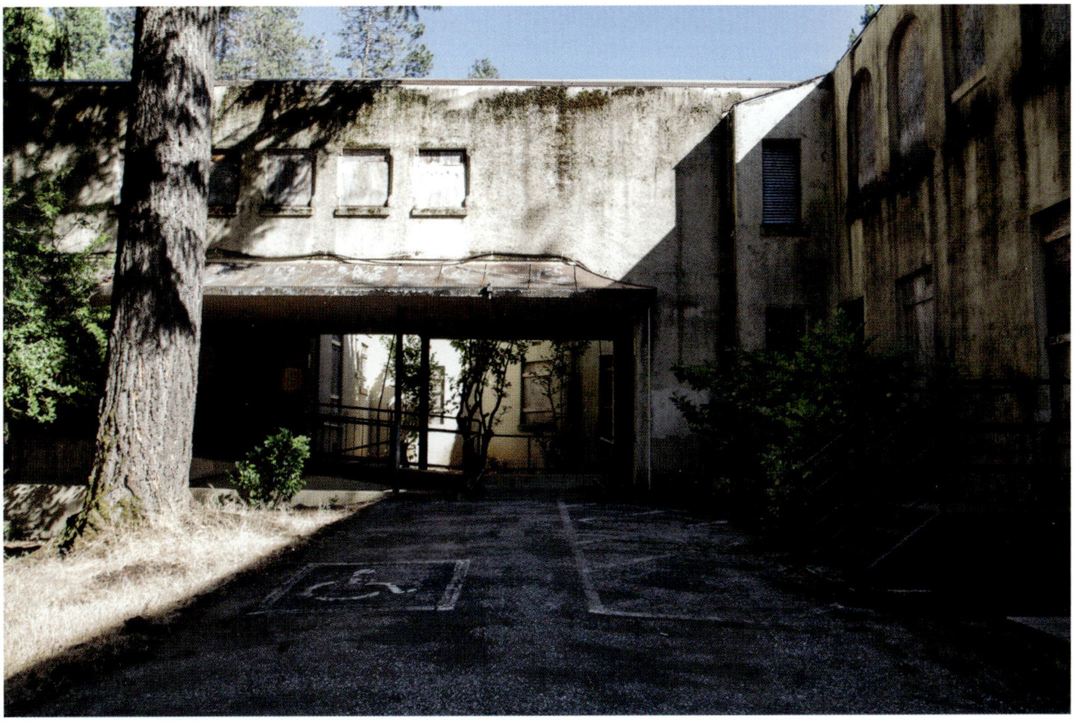

Walking into the grounds of the hospital.

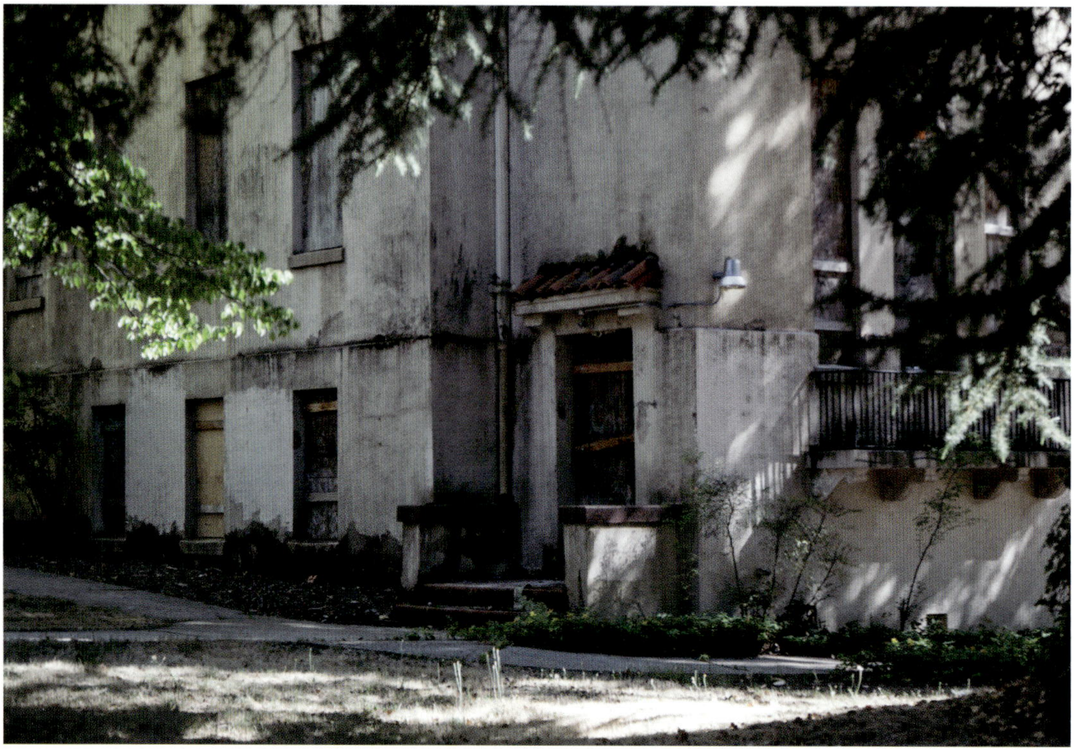

An exterior wall and entrance to the Nevada County Hospital.

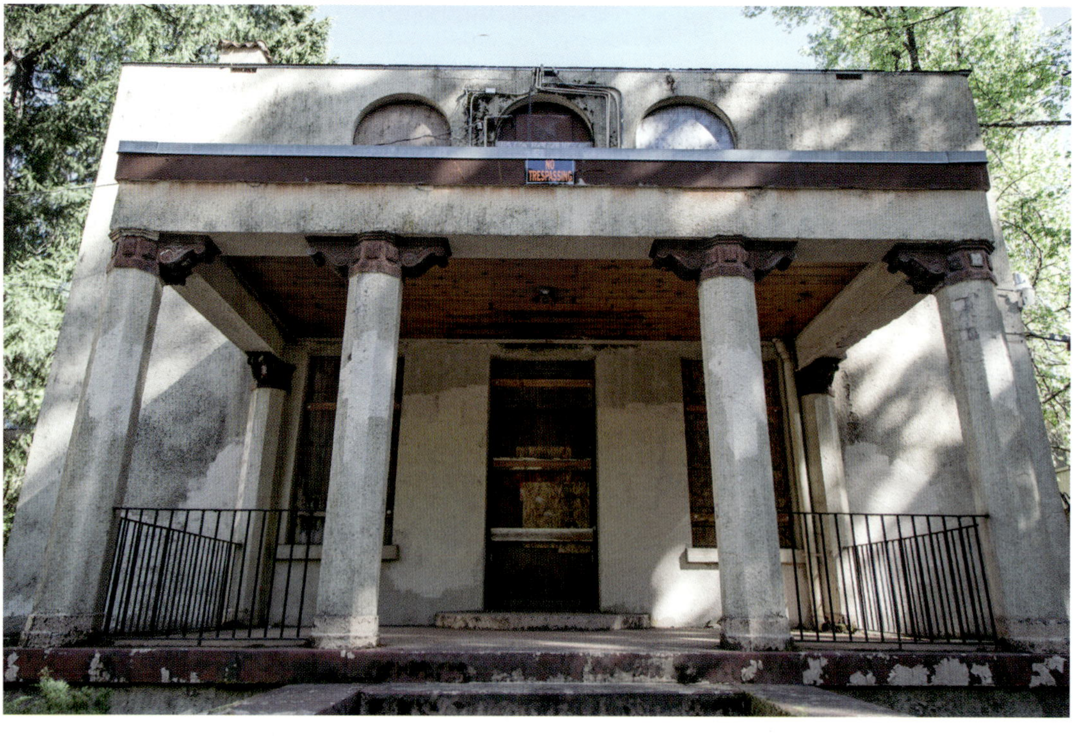

"No Trespassing" signs are posted throughout the hospital grounds.

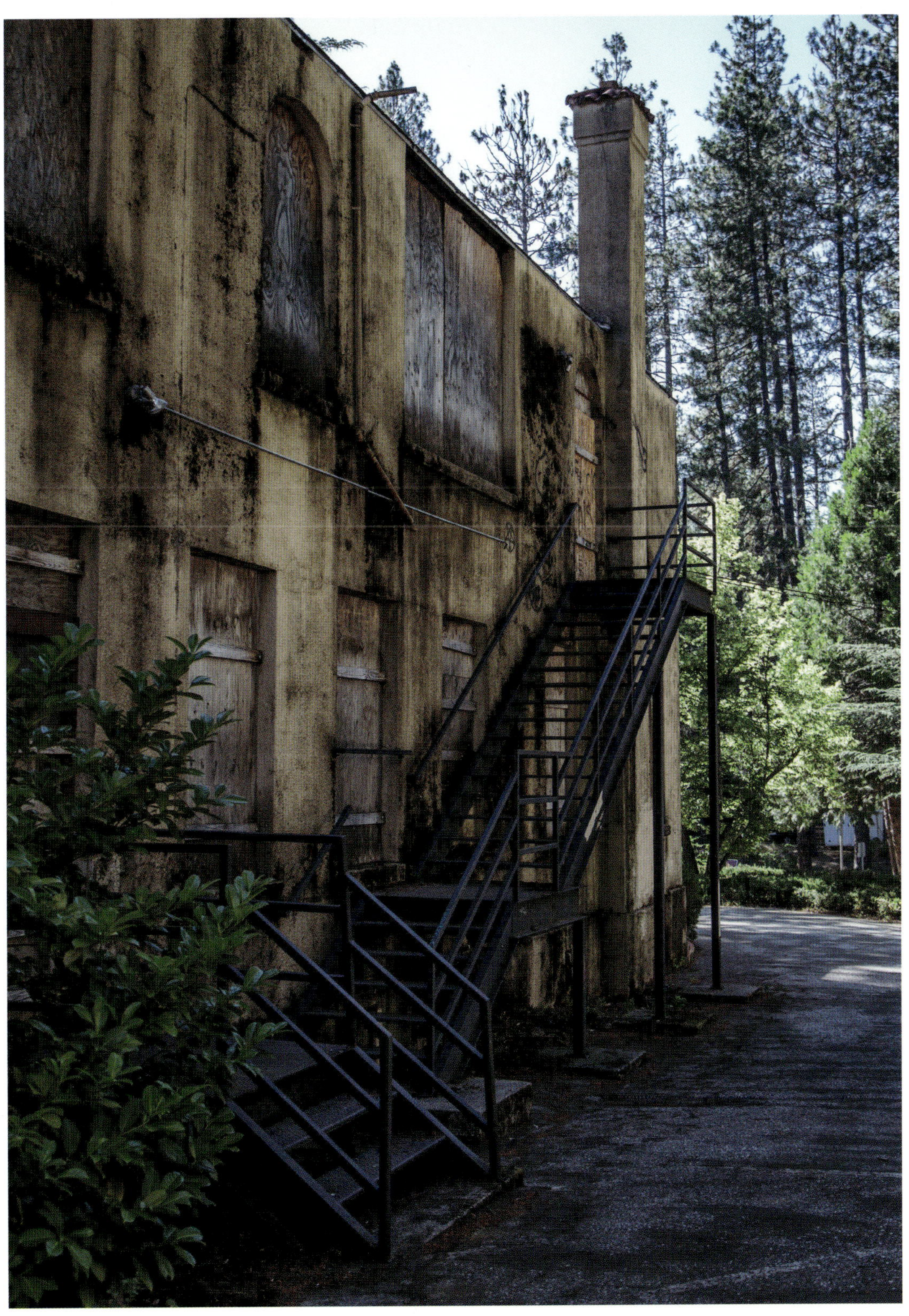

The aging and rusting process has already started to take effect at Nevada County Hospital.

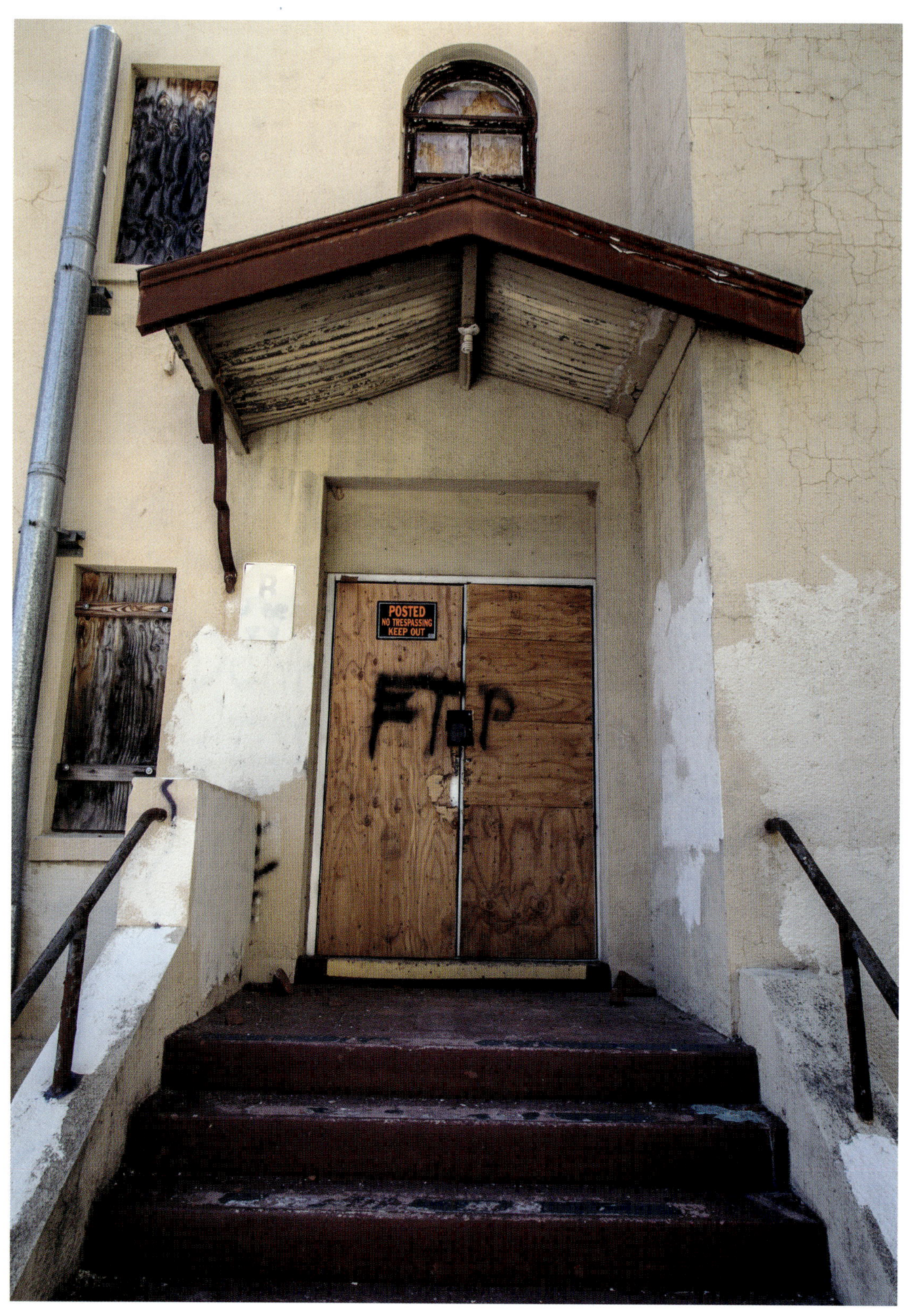

A close up of one of the hospital's entrances, all sealed shut.

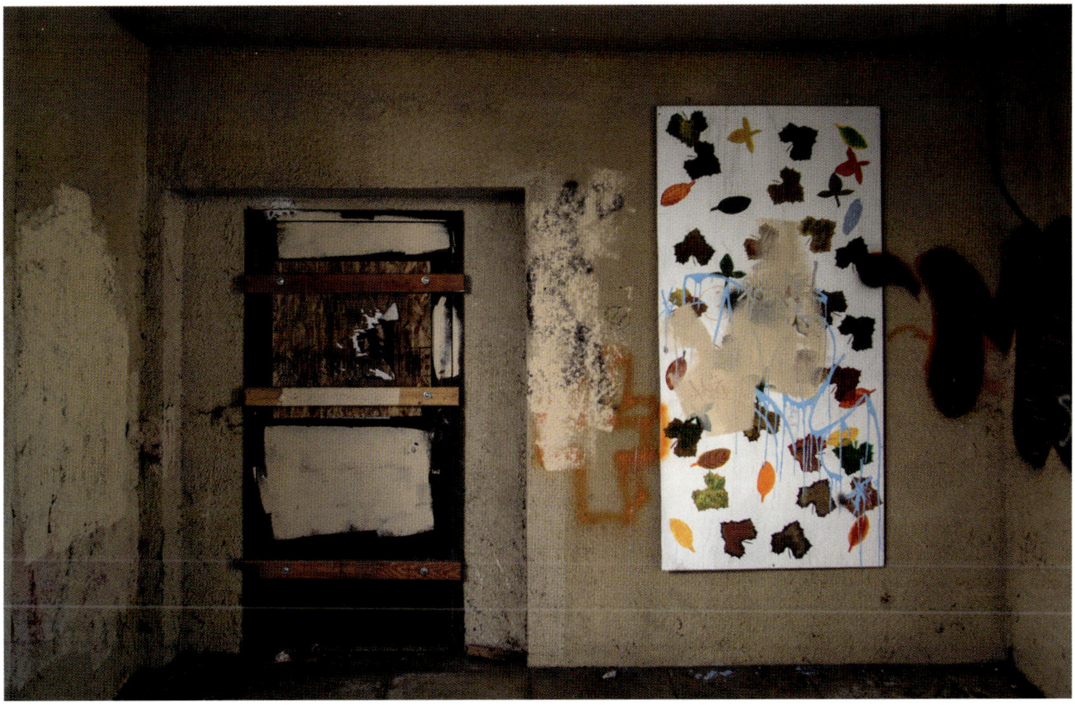

A once-colorful mural now sits abandoned.

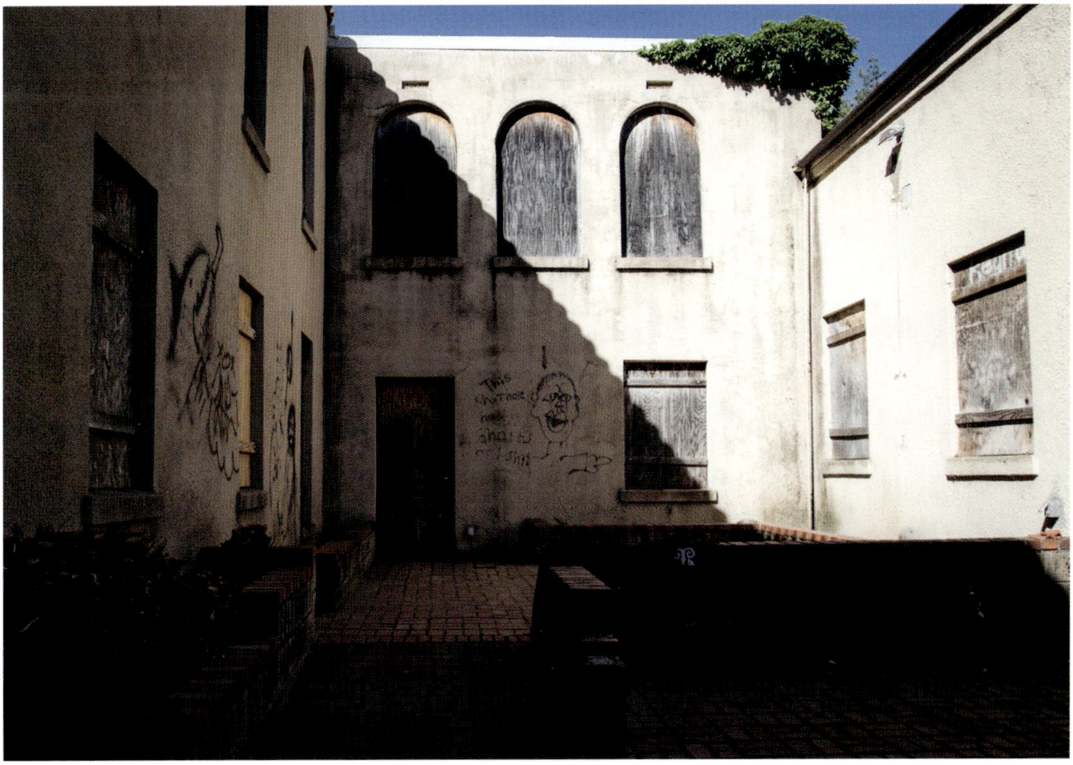

A courtyard of the hospital, with graffiti mentioning ghosts in the background.

7

ABANDONED NORTHERN CALIFORNIA: A LAND OF CONTRADICTIONS

It's hard to believe that there is a place in the US where within a couple of hours' drive, you can find sprawling military bases, immense wineries, gold mining towns, and amusement parks all lying abandoned. Yet Northern California encompasses all these odd combinations of different people and industries, and many more.

The ruins that lie in the area today reflect the various ways people attempted to build their future in Northern California—not unlike the innovative ways people still try to build their future in the area today, whether that involves a cool new start-up, a prominent position in the local, internationally-respected wine industry, or seeking inspiration for an amazing new book in the redwood forests of the Sierras.

If there is one thing that this cross-section of humanity had in common, it was the will to forge ahead into the unknown. Inventors, military men, gold prospectors, entrepreneurs—they all, in their own ways, took their risks and chances in this newer part of the USA, to create a life, a business, a work of art, or miracle of science that had never been done before. This is the proud, vibrant legacy left to Northern California today.

BIBLIOGRAPHY

"16th Street Station." *Atlas Obscura.* https://www.atlasobscura.com/places/16th-street-train-station-oakland Accessed July 3, 2018.

"Abandoned Nevada County Hospital: The Historic and Tragic Tale of the HEW Building." *Calexplornia.* http://www.calexplornia.com/abandoned-nevada-county-hospital-the-historic-and-tragic-tale-of-the-hew-building/ Accessed July 2, 2018.

Balicki, Janet. "Explore the History of Bay Area Ghost Towns." *Press Democrat.* December 1, 2016. http://www.pressdemocrat.com/lifestyle/6370935-181/explore-the-history-of-bay?sba=AAS.

Cogswell, Ned. "12 Historic Events That Shaped San Francisco." *The Culture Trip.* October 20, 2016. https://theculturetrip.com/north-america/usa/california/articles/12-historical-events-that-shaped-san-francisco.

"Donner Pass Summit Tunnels." *Atlas Obscura.* https://www.atlasobscura.com/places/donner-pass-summit-tunnels Accessed July 6, 2018.

"Former Naval Station Treasure Island." *Naval Facilities Engineering Command.* https://www.bracpmo.navy.mil/brac_bases/california/former_ns_treasure_island.html Accessed July 5, 2018.

"Fort Baker: Battery Spencer." *Military Museum.* http://www.militarymuseum.org/BtySpencer.html Accessed July 7, 2018.

Fronistas, Phoebe. "Richmond's Historic Winehaven Building The Early Center of California Wine Industry." *East Bay Times.* October 16, 2009. https://www.eastbaytimes.com/2009/10/16/richmonds-historic-winehaven-building-the-early-center-of-california-wine-industry.

"J's Amusement Park and Haunted House." *Lost America.* https://lostamerica.com/photo-items/js-amusement-park-and-haunted-house/ Accessed June 30, 2018.

"Jack London Grave Site and Wolf House." *Jack London State Historic Park.*

http://jacklondonpark.com/jack-london-docent-grave-site-wolf-house.html Accessed July 3, 2018.

Kelly, Debra. "Abandoned Military Structures on Treasure Island, San Francisco Bay." *Urban Ghosts*. July 1, 2016. https://www.urbanghostsmedia.com/2016/07/abandoned-treasure-island-san-francisco.

"The Marconi Hotel." *Atlas Obscura*. https://www.atlasobscura.com/places/the-marconi-hotel Accessed July 10, 2018.

"Laura's Law in Nevada County: A Model for Action – Saving Money and Lives." *Nevada County Court*. http://nccourt.net/documents/gjreports/1112-HEV-AB-1421LaurasLaw.pdf Accessed July 10, 2018.

"Naval Station, Treasure Island." *Military Museum*. http://www.militarymuseum.org/NSTI.html Accessed July 7, 2018.

"NPL Site Narrative for Alameda Naval Air Station." *National Priorities List*. United States Environmental Protection Agency. February 24, 2006. https://cumulis.epa.gov/supercpad/cursites/csitinfo.cfm?id=0902731.

Piatt, Michael H. "Bodie: The Mines Are Looking Well…" *Bodie History*. http://www.bodiehistory.com/bodie.htm Accessed July 6, 2018.

Prado, Mark. "Decades-old shipwreck off Point Reyes identified by NOAA effort." *Marinij,* September 16, 2014. http://www.marinij.com/article/zz/20140916/NEWS/140917742.